Becoming

LESSONS OF WISDOM FROM
THE BOOK OF PROVERBS

CARRIE D. ROGERS

Table of Contents

Introduction

"The most important thing in your life is not what you do; it's who you become."
— Dallas Willard

How much thought do you give to the person you're *becoming*? Or maybe a better first question is this: What do you think about when you read the word *becoming*?

Do you think about traits you want to see more of in your life — like becoming wiser, more gracious, or more clear in purpose? Or do you think about the things you'd like to see less — like becoming less fearful, less envious, or less focused on self?

The dictionary defines *becoming* as "to come, change, or grow to be," which covers both our mores and lesses. To me, *becoming* is about leaning into a process — it's a continual forming, shaping, and growing to become the person we were created to be.

In the Bible, the apostle Paul speaks clearly about *becoming* in his letter to the church in Philippi:

> I am confident that the Creator, who has begun such a great work among you, *will not stop in mid-design but will keep perfecting you* until the day Jesus the Anointed, our Liberating King, returns to redeem the world.
> (Philippians 1:6 THE VOICE)

Did you catch that? Paul teaches us that God — the One who dreamed us up, crafted, and created us — won't give up on us mid-design. He promises to keep working in us, perfecting us until the day we meet Him face-to-face.

While you and I are still living on this side of eternity, there's no such thing as arriving. *Arriving* is a myth. It's a tease — a recipe for discontentment and endless striving. A decade or two ago, this truth may have disappointed me, but today I'm relieved.

I'm relieved that there's no such thing as knowing it all, and I'm delighted that I don't have to have it all figured out, boxed up, and presented with a shiny, pink bow.

5

Instead, you and I are called to settle ourselves into the pursuit of continually *becoming.* In this pursuit, we're called to lean into a beautiful, hands-on, character-shaping, glory-making process as Jesus makes and molds us from the inside out, one baby step at a time.

I want to live a *becoming* life, and I hope you do, too.

That's where the Book of Proverbs comes in.

The Book of Proverbs is a collection of wise statements, called proverbs, written primarily by Solomon (the wisest man who ever lived). Each proverb gives practical insight and guidelines for how to live well in life and in relation to others.

Listen to how pastor and teacher Raymond C. Ortlund Jr. introduces the Book of Proverbs in his book *Proverbs: Wisdom That Works*: "Everyone is on a path. Everyone is going somewhere. When we feel stuck, even when we feel trapped, the truth is, we are still in motion. Life is a journey, and the end of it all is not just a place but also a condition. We are *becoming* the end of our journey, wise or foolish, and every moment takes us closer there. ... Through the Book of Proverbs, God coaches us in the *wisdom* we need throughout the long and complicated path of our everyday lives."[1]

Obviously, you and I won't be able to cover everything in this vast book of knowledge. This is not a comprehensive study of the Book of Proverbs, but rather a topical approach to understanding, learning, and growing through the wisdom the book provides.

Like most devotionals, each day's material includes:

- Key Scripture
- Devotional
- Prayer

In each daily read, you and I will look to the proverbs for practical wisdom as we walk out our everyday realities in this ongoing process of becoming. And as we lean into one proverb at a time, we will not only learn to take in and apply godly wisdom for right living, but we will also come face-to-face with the daily reality of our desperate need for Jesus.

Additionally, unlike other devotionals, the format of this book invites us to pick up a fork and dig into Scripture for ourselves. Therefore, it also contains two additional sections:

- **GRAB YOUR FORK.** This section contains reflection questions based on the devotion to help you think critically and practically apply the proverb to your own life.

- **HUNGRY FOR MORE?** This section takes the lesson a step further, connecting and expanding the text with other Scripture. My desire for this section is that it will grow in us a hunger for more of God's Word.

At the end of each week, I offer a simple review of each week's material, plus space for us to reflect on and seal in the lessons we've learned — because in the end, it's not about checking the boxes and closing the book; it's about deepening our trust and leaning more fully into Jesus, our faithful Guide and Friend.

Unless noted, all Scripture is NIV, and all definitions are from dictionary.com.

[1]Ortlund, Raymond C. Jr. *Proverbs: Wisdom That Works.* Wheaton, IL: Crossway, 2012, 15.

Wisdom

*The fear of the Lord is the beginning of knowledge, but
fools despise wisdom and discipline.*
Proverbs 1:7

1
The Source

For the LORD gives wisdom, and from
his mouth come knowledge and understanding.
Proverbs 2:6

Some words, like *wisdom*, are tricky to define. In my head, I know what it is. And given a list of choices, I'd like to believe I can recognize what it's not. However, it's difficult for me to wrap simple words around the concept of wisdom, let alone tie it up with a neat and tidy bow.

For starters, I know that wisdom is more than being smart. It's more than acquiring additional information and loading our heads with endless knowledge. Growing in knowledge is important, but without wisdom knowledge is useless.

According to the dictionary, *wisdom* is "the quality of being wise; knowledge of what is true or right coupled with just judgment as to action; discernment or insight."

Listen to how King Solomon introduces his book of wisdom in Proverbs 1:1–6:

> The proverbs of Solomon son of David, king of Israel:
> ² for attaining wisdom and discipline;
>   for understanding words of insight;
> ³ for acquiring a disciplined and prudent life,
>   doing what is right and just and fair;
> ⁴ for giving prudence to the simple,
>   knowledge and discretion to the young—
> ⁵ let the wise listen and add to their learning,
>   and let the discerning get guidance—
> ⁶ for understanding proverbs and parables,
>   the sayings and riddles of the wise.

From this passage, we glean that wisdom includes much more than head knowledge. Wisdom is knowing how to live a disciplined life, how to make wise choices, and how to do the right thing at the right time in life and in relation to others. It's both the ability to discern what is best and the strength of character to live it out.

Wisdom understands how life works well and lives accordingly.

When I read Solomon's words about wisdom, my interest is piqued. I want to be a woman of wisdom, and because you're reading this devotional, I assume the same is true for you.

The question now is, how do we get it?

Today's key verse gives us our answer. God is the Source of all wisdom. There is no wisdom apart from Him. All wisdom is revealed and imparted by the Giver of all good things (James 1:17).

Yes, even in this information age of Siri, Alexa, and Google, still nothing compares to the wisdom of the Lord.

> ... from his mouth come knowledge and understanding. (Proverbs 2:6b)

I don't know about you, but I've never heard the audible voice of God imparting wisdom to me from heaven. However, I've learned we can hear God's words in two primary ways: the *written* Word of God and the *living* Word of God.

#1: THE WRITTEN WORD OF GOD: THE BIBLE

The Bible is unlike any other book we will ever read. It isn't merely a collection of stories or ideas about God — it's the very Word of God. Although written by the hands of men, each word was inspired, or breathed, by God Himself (2 Timothy 3:16).

I love this often-quoted piece of advice: "If you want to hear God speak, read the Bible. If you want to hear Him speak audibly, read it out loud."

Scripture is the primary way God speaks to us. When we read God's Word, the Holy Spirit impresses His truth on our hearts in ways that teach, correct, and transform us forever. The more we devote ourselves to reading and applying the Scriptures, the more we will grow in wisdom.

#2: THE LIVING WORD OF GOD: JESUS

The Gospel of John describes Jesus as the Word made flesh (John 1:14). Jesus is the full revelation of God with skin on. Not only that, but He's also called the very wisdom of God (1 Corinthians 1:30).

Wisdom

11

No one knows the mind of God (His wisdom, understanding, and truth) except God Himself. When we become spiritually alive (by believing in and receiving Jesus into our lives), God imparts His wisdom to us personally through the Holy Spirit from the inside out (1 Corinthians 2:10-13).

The more we learn to live our lives with Jesus, walking and talking with Him daily in prayer, the more He will, through the Holy Spirit, live His wisdom through you and me.

GRAB YOUR FORK

Whom or what do you usually turn to when you want/need wisdom?

Of the two ways we hear from God, the written Word and the living Word, which do you want to grow in most?

What do you need wisdom for today?

PRAYER

Heavenly Father, thank You for revealing Yourself as the Source of all wisdom. As I lean into this process of becoming, remind me throughout the day to turn to You for wisdom, and give me the courage and conviction to act on the wisdom You give. Grow in me a genuine desire for Your Word, Lord. I want to hear from You.

HUNGRY FOR MORE?

Read 2 Chronicles 1:7–12. What did Solomon ask for from God? How did God respond?

Although God gave Solomon wisdom, Solomon didn't always act upon His wisdom. Our wisdom is never perfectly applied, even when perfectly given.[1] Can you think of a time when although you knew the wise choice, you decided to choose another way instead?

Read James 3:13–18. How does this definition of heavenly wisdom differ from the world's view of wisdom?

How do these verses in James 3 give us a picture of Jesus?

One powerful way to grow in wisdom is to pray God's Word back to Him. Read Daniel 2:20–23. Use Daniel's words in this passage to write out your own prayer of praise in faith to the Giver of all wisdom today.

2
First Things First

The fear of the Lord is the beginning of wisdom,
and knowledge of the Holy One is understanding.
Proverbs 9:10

Ask anyone in the construction industry, and they'll tell you the most important part of a house's structure is the foundation. Laying a proper foundation is the most essential part of the entire building process. If a home is built upon a strong and stable foundation, it can stand for years to come.

Keep this idea in your mind as you read today's key verse. The fear of the Lord is the beginning of wisdom like the foundation of a house is the beginning of a house. The fear of the Lord is what wisdom is built upon. Just as you can't have a stable house without investing in a solid foundation, you can't have wisdom without a fear of the Lord.

Let's break down some of the words in this verse so we can have a better understanding of the proverb's meaning. First, the word *beginning* means "the foundation, prerequisite, first thing." So, the first and most important step in becoming wise is a proper view of and relationship with God. Wisdom is for those who *fear the Lord*.

When you hear the words "fear of the Lord," don't think of a shaky, scared fear like you've seen a ghost or a monster. Instead, think about it this way: If you were sitting on your bed at night and heard the big, booming voice of God speaking down to you from heaven, how would you feel?

An experience like that would be amazing and downright terrifying, right? I think it's fair to say we would all be afraid. However, the fear we'd experience wouldn't be because God is bad or mean or threatening. We'd be shaking because God is big and powerful and mind-blowingly awesome. *That's* the fear of the Lord.

But still, there's more to the fear of the Lord than our emotional response to Him. Taken one step further, the fear of the Lord can also be understood as worshipping submission.[2] Those who fear

Wisdom

Lord understand who God is, live in awe of His power, and obey His Word. They properly submit themselves to His holy nature, His divine authority, and His sovereign right to rule, not out of obligation but out of love.

To put it simply, they have a proper understanding of who God is (and who they're not) and respond accordingly.

Scripture teaches us that wisdom is always revealed in a relationship that lives in awe of and submission to God because He is good and faithful and trustworthy. It continues to grow, build, and mature over time through discipleship — in living and walking with Jesus, who is the very wisdom of God (1 Corinthians 1:30).

One of my favorite verses is Psalm 25:14:

> The LORD confides in those who fear him; he makes his covenant known to them.

Picture two friends sitting on a couch, sharing secrets and enjoying time together. That's the picture this verse paints for us. Oh, to be one the Lord confides in! To receive His wise counsel and understand His ways. I can't think of anything better.

GRAB YOUR FORK

In the past, what has been your understanding and experience of the "fear of the Lord"?

Why do you think the Lord gives wisdom (or confides in) those who fear Him?

If wisdom is found in a relationship with Jesus, list some ways that we can invest in our relationship with Him.

Which of these is your favorite way to personally spend time with Jesus?

PRAYER

Father God, I believe by faith that every time I open my Bible, hungry for more of You, You will reveal Yourself to me. Would You grow my perspective and understanding of You? Remind me often of Your goodness and faithfulness, and assure me that my surrender is well placed in You. Please grow in me a heart of worshipping submission — an immovable foundation that wisdom can be built upon.

HUNGRY FOR MORE?

The first biblical reference to the fear of God appears in Genesis when God tests Abraham in the sacrifice of his son Isaac. Read Genesis 22:1–14, specifically verse 12. How do you think our fear of God corresponds to our trust (or faith) in Him?

Read Isaiah 11:1–3. This prophetic passage foretells of Jesus as our coming Messiah. The Message version of verse 3 says, "Fear-of-God will be all his joy and delight." How does Jesus' life prove His delight in honoring and obeying His Father?

Some translations use the word *obey* in place of the word *fear*. How does this change the meaning of the word *fear* for you? How do you think our fear of God affects our obedience to Him?

How does Solomon's concluding statement in Ecclesiastes 12:13 restate (and reinforce) the connection between the fear of God and obedience?

In what areas of your life right now are you challenged to trust and obey God more?

3
Seek and Find

Blessed is the man who listens to me,
watching daily at my doors, waiting at my doorway.
For whoever finds me finds life and receives favor from the LORD.
Proverbs 8:34-35

It's only Day 3 and we've already touched on two foundational truths in becoming wise, but there's one more important piece we need to uncover.

In Day 1 we learned that God is the Giver of all wisdom. There is no wisdom apart from Him. In Day 2 we learned that our ability to receive this wisdom requires two things. First, God gives wisdom to those who live in a thriving, God-fearing relationship with Him. Today we'll focus on the second: God gives wisdom to those who earnestly seek it. Wisdom is gifted to us when we pursue it.

So, what exactly does it mean (or look like) to seek the Lord for wisdom? Proverbs 2:1-4 offers some practical instructions for seeking wisdom. Read the passage (written for you below) from THE VOICE translation:

> [1] My son, if you accept what I am telling you
> and store my counsel and directives deep within
> you,
> [2] If you listen for Lady Wisdom, attune your ears to
> her, and engage your mind to understand what she
> is telling you,
> [3] If you cry out to her for insight
> and beg for understanding,
> [4] If you sift through the clamor of everything around you
> to seek her like some precious prize,
> to search for her like buried treasure;

Let's break this passage down, piece by piece, so that we can understand and apply it accordingly.

RECEIVE AND STORE (VERSE 1)

This is the message of any teacher to his student: Take my teaching seriously. Don't waste your time merely running your eyes across the pages of truth. Instead, receive it. Take it in. Let my words sink into the very fiber of your being.

We do this by immersing ourselves in Scripture. We read it — study it — meditate on it and memorize it. Try thinking of it as affixing the Word of God like wallpaper to your heart, mind, and soul.

LISTEN AND APPLY (VERSE 2)

You and I both know that there's a world of difference between *hearing* and *listening*. When I give my children instructions, I expect them to listen carefully to what I say and then put what they hear into action. The same is true when receiving instruction from the Lord. Listening implies obedience. It's putting our trust into action. Wisdom grows when we learn to do what God says.

Additionally, to turn our ear to wisdom, we must be willing to turn away from the words/voices of others. By nature, to say yes to one voice is to say no to another. So, who currently has your ear? Whose words do you most readily listen to? If we want to grow in wisdom, God's Word and God's voice must take precedence. When we do this, God will honor our commitment and bless us with His presence, protection, and provision (Proverbs 2:6-8).

I love how verse 2 then says "engage your mind to understand." We not only have the ability but also the responsibility to think and act upon what we're reading. No matter what season of life or stage we're in, we can be students — or thinkers — of the Word. God can and will make us smarter and wiser than we really are when we learn to listen and apply His Word to our everyday lives.

PURSUE (VERSES 3-4)

Can you see the progression of the author's pursuit in these verses? Cry out. Beg for. Sift through. Seek. Search. Growing in wisdom isn't automatic. We will never grow wiser by coasting. We must be willing to sift through the noise and dig down deep to uncover truth.

Because, as this passage tells us, if we search for wisdom, we will find it. God is always faithful to His Word.

> Then you will understand what it means to fear the LORD, and you will gain knowledge of God.
> For the LORD grants wisdom! From his mouth come knowledge and understanding.
> (Proverbs 2:5–6 NLT)

Wisdom is found when we learn to pause and turn to Jesus. Maybe the simple answer to many of our looming questions is: We do not have because we do not ask (James 4:2).

GRAB YOUR FORK

When was the last time you sought the Lord for wisdom? What was it for?

Think through each of these three "steps" of seeking …

RECEIVE AND STORE: Who currently has your ear? Whose words do you most readily listen to (the news, popular social media opinions, your own thoughts, your family members, friends, Google, etc.)?

What has been your experience with Scripture memory? How do you think memorizing Scripture can give us wisdom?

LISTEN AND APPLY: Do you consider yourself a student of God's Word? If not, what's holding you back (for example, disinterest, fear, insecurity, lack of time, or something else)? Would you be willing to give it a try?

Wisdom

PURSUE: If you had to rate your pursuit of God (and the wisdom He gives) on a scale of 1–5, where are you today?

Try this ... No matter where you are, resolve to seek the Lord daily by committing to this devotional. Decide you're going to dig in and do the work. There are no shortcuts to knowing God and growing in wisdom. Maybe leaning into the Lord through this little book will be one way for you to seek Him more.

PRAYER

Father God, thank You for the promise that when we seek You, we will find You. Please instill in me the discipline to keep my eyes focused on You, my ears attuned to Your voice, and my heart inclined to Your purposes. I want to live my life in a continual pursuit of You.

HUNGRY FOR MORE?

Re-read today's key verse. Who is the "me" this verse is referring to? (It may help to look up the verse in your Bible for more context.) What are the rewards for the finders?

How does James 1:5 echo the truths we learned today?

Psalm 119, the longest of all the psalms, is all about the beauty and importance of God's Word. Read Psalm 119:97–104. List at least three benefits the psalmist gives for reading/studying the Bible.

4
The Fool

The fear of the LORD is the beginning of knowledge,
but fools despise wisdom and discipline.
Proverbs 1:7

What is the opposite of being wise? If you answered "dumb," you're on the right track. However, in the same way that wisdom is more than being smart, there is a word that means more than dumb. That word is *foolish*. Thankfully, the Book of Proverbs helps us understand what a fool is so that we don't become one.

In this world, there is wisdom and there is folly (or foolishness). As we've already learned, wisdom begins with a knowledge and fear of God. The wise aren't scared of God because they think He's a mean, unfair ruler. Rather, they live in awe of Him because they know Him as a loving, faithful, and merciful Father. The wise understand that all wisdom comes from God, so they listen to Him carefully and do what He says.

The Bible paints a very different picture of a fool. The fool says in his heart there is no God and sees no need for Him. They are the kind of people who live for themselves, trust only in themselves, and determine their own right and wrong. They hate instruction and throw away correction, especially when it comes to the Word of God. Folly isn't being silly. In fact, it's sinful.

In Psalm 14:1, the psalmist David writes, "A fool says in his heart, 'There is no God.' " In this verse, David acknowledges the utter foolishness of creation to turn its back on the Creator. Only a fool would deny the existence of and his need for God.

While it might be easy for us to point fingers at modern-day atheists, let's be careful before we call someone a fool (Matthew 5:22). There are a couple other details for us to consider.

1. In the original language, "there is" does not exist. The verse, then, could be read, "A fool says in his heart, 'NO God!' " Could this mean that anytime we say no to God and go our own way, we too would be considered a fool?

Wisdom

2. The saying "says in his heart" implies that perhaps the heart can say one thing while the lips say something different. Could this be saying that though our mouths profess faith, our lives may prove the opposite?

I think I just stepped on my own toes. How often do I deny God's existence by going my own selfish way? Does the way I live my life prove my faith or deny God's existence?

I can think of several times specifically in the last several years that I told God "NO" in my professional life by telling Him "I'll never." "God, I really like writing, but I'll never speak." And then, "OK, fine. I'll speak, but I'm never going to make teaching videos." I learned very quickly that if I want to grow — if I want to continually walk closely with the Lord — my life will have to become a living "YES" to Him. Anything else is foolishness.

GRAB YOUR FORK

According to what you just learned, what is the main difference between the wise and the fool?

For most of us, it's not God's existence we deny. It's our desperate need for Him that we miss. Think through every part of your life (things like your relationships, marriage, parenting, occupation, health, finances, etc.). What areas of your life might you be living as though you don't need God?

In what ways have you said NO to God recently? What have been the consequences?

In what ways have you said YES to God recently? What have been the consequences?

PRAYER

Lord, forgive me for my foolish ways — for the areas of my life where I'm challenged to believe in the reality of Your existence (Your power, Your authority, and Your right to rule). Open my eyes to see my folly for what it is, and open my heart to receive more of You. I want my life to be a living "YES" to You in all I say and do.

HUNGRY FOR MORE?

Look up the following verses and note how each describes the fool.

Proverbs 14:9

Proverbs 18:2

Proverbs 18:6–7

Proverbs 26:11

Proverbs 28:26

Read Titus 3:3–8. In case any of us were feeling self-righteous regarding foolishness, what is the one and only reason any of us can become wise?

Wisdom

5
What Will You Choose?

Does not wisdom call out? Does not understanding raise her voice?
"To you, O men, I call out; I raise my voice to all mankind.
You who are simple, gain prudence; you who are
foolish, gain understanding."
Proverbs 8:1, 4–5

I don't know about you, but usually by the time the weekend arrives, I'm burned out on decision making. What's for dinner? What are we going to do today? Please don't make me decide. In this world overloaded with options, the struggle of decision fatigue is real.

Thankfully in the Book of Proverbs, our choices are limited to only two. Proverbs 9 tells the story of two women who live in houses on opposite sides of the street. Each woman has prepared a meal and is inviting all who will listen to join her for dinner. Whose voice will we listen to? Which house will we choose?

The first voice we hear in Proverbs 9:1–6 is that of **LADY WISDOM**. Not only has she prepared a delicious feast, a banquet of all her best, but she also has decorated her home and laid out fine china. Her offer is to all who wish to dine with her, "Come! Enjoy dinner with me, and learn to live a life with meaning."

In Proverbs 9:13–18, from the other side of the street, we hear another voice, loud and strangely intoxicating. This is the voice of **MADAM FOLLY**. She too has prepared a meal and invites all who will listen to come in and eat. However, instead of fine dining, Madam Folly is throwing a wild party and offering only stolen food. She makes big promises that sound sweet, but her words are only lies.

When I read the invitations of these two voices, the right choice seems obvious; however, I've lived long enough to know that it's not that simple. The truth is, we are complicated people with histories, scars, and wounds from the past. Not only that, but our hearts are deceptive — bent toward sin (Jeremiah 17:9). Our wills are stubborn. Our emotions are bossy. If we're honest, we spend much of our time running back and forth between the two houses.

Plus most of the time, the wise choice doesn't come to us in neon, flashing lights. "I'm wise. Pick me!" Similarly, the way of the fool usually isn't dripping with darkness and deceit. So how do we know? In a moment's notice, when both voices are calling, how do we decide?

The not-so-simple answer lies in the truth we discovered in our first two days together. Wisdom is always received in relationship. There is no wisdom apart from God. So with each choice, we picture Jesus smiling and waving from the doorway of Lady Wisdom's grand home. "Come in!" He says, extending His hand. "Come in. Sit and eat. Let's talk it out together. I'll show you what to do."

GRAB YOUR FORK

Do you ever suffer from decision fatigue? When is it most difficult for you to make decisions?

Can you think of a time when you thought you were making the wise choice, but in the end, you realized you were only being entertained by folly? Share about it here.

Is this how you picture Jesus — as the wisest of all your friends — ready and willing to share godly advice with you? Why or why not?

How could viewing Jesus this way help you in becoming wise?

PRAYER

Father God, in this process of becoming, teach me how to walk closely with Jesus, who is faithful to live wisdom in and through me by the power of the Holy Spirit. Steer my heart away from the house of folly. I want to make choices that are shaped by my love and trust in You.

HUNGRY FOR MORE?

Read the following passages, and answer the questions below.

- Proverbs 1:20–32
- Romans 1:18–25

How is a fool described in these verses (Proverbs 1:24–25, 29–30; Romans 1:21–23)?

What are the consequences of foolishness (Proverbs 1:31–32; Romans 1:24–25)?

If wisdom is so readily available, why do you think so many people choose foolishness?

WEEK ONE: *Recap and Reflection*

DAY 1
God is the Source of all wisdom.

DAY 2
God gives wisdom to those who fear Him.

DAY 3
God gives wisdom to those who seek Him.

DAY 4
The fool is someone who denies the existence of and need for the Lord.

DAY 5
The choice between wisdom and folly is ours. What will you choose?

What is one thing you learned about God this week?

How does this new truth point you to Jesus?

[1]Gwendolyn Lau, my theological mentor.
[2]Kidner, David. *Proverbs.* Downers Grove, IL: InterVarsity Press, 1964, p. 56.

Pride

When pride comes, then comes disgrace,
but with humility comes wisdom.
Proverbs 11:2

6
What Is Pride?

Do you see a man wise in his own eyes?
There is more hope for a fool than for him.
Proverbs 26:12

I'm entering this week with an extra measure of prayer. Some of the hardest lessons I've learned in life have had to do with the topic of pride. While it's true that some lessons are best learned the hard way, these lessons on pride are worth learning by instruction and example, if we are willing.

The dictionary defines *pride* as "a high or inordinate opinion of one's own dignity, importance, merit, or superiority, whether as cherished in the mind or as displayed in bearing, conduct, etc." To me, pride is when I think, speak, or act like the world revolves around me, myself, and I. Pride is big-headed and conceited, always looking out for number one.

I've learned, however, that there's more to pride than having all eyes on the ever-important me. Pride can also be disguised as something virtuous and maybe even admirable.

In the world today, we're taught to strive for self-sufficiency, self-confidence, and self-reliance. Living as an independent woman who can do it all *and* keep it all together seems like a worthy goal. But when we trust in ourselves, grasp for control, and live without acknowledging our need for God, it's important to recognize that pride has snuck its way in.

Psalm 10:4 says,

> In his pride the wicked does not seek him; in all his thoughts there is no room for God.

Sadly, this verse often describes me. Early this week when my boy came down with a fever, my first thoughts were consumed with me, myself, and I. Instinctively I grabbed my calendar and to-do list and worried over how I could possibly get any writing done with a sick kid at home. After vain attempts to readjust my schedule came the task of personally diagnosing my child's illness. In pride, I didn't stop to seek the Lord. Instead, I grabbed the reins of control, searched Google, and called a friend. In all my thoughts, there was no room for God.

This psalm reminds me of a quote from Charles Spurgeon, "As long as man is full of himself, he leaves no room for Jesus."

In God's economy, there's no such thing as a self-sufficient, independent follower of Jesus. We were all created to live fully dependent on the Lord for everything we do, just as Jesus did (John 5:19). Anything less is prideful. Any time we hear that inner voice that says, "My way is best. I don't need God's help on this one," we need to be careful! Pride is looming at our door.

GRAB YOUR FORK

How do you define pride?

Have you ever thought of having an independent spirit as prideful? Why or why not?

Re-read today's key verse. In what ways are you wise in your own eyes?

What are some ways we can practice making more room in our thoughts for God?

PRAYER

Father, forgive me for thinking far too much about me. I humble myself before You today and ask that You would cut away the pride in my life. You are my Creator, Sustainer, and everything I need. Apart from You, I can do nothing of eternal value. Thank You for walking out this journey of becoming with me.

HUNGRY FOR MORE?

Read Isaiah 14:12–15 and Ezekiel 28:12–19. Although these passages were written about earthly kings, they both describe Satan's sin and rebellion. Ultimately, what was the cause of his downfall? And what was his punishment?

Read John 15:1–6. How does the analogy of the vine and the branches give us a picture of what healthy dependence on Jesus looks like?

7

Pride's Consequence

Pride goes before destruction,
a haughty spirit before a fall.
Proverbs 16:18

Although I'm certainly not a parenting expert, I've learned over the years that my children often learn best when I allow them to experience the natural consequences of their choices. Natural consequences are the experiences that naturally follow a choice or behavior. For example, in the winter if my child forgets his coat when he runs out the door to school in the morning, he will probably be cold at recess. Every choice, whether positive or negative, has a consequence.

When it comes to pride, we don't have to look further than the most basic laws of physics to know the consequence that's eventually coming. After all, what goes up must come down.[1]

From cover to cover, the Bible is clear about God's stance on pride *and* its consequence.

> The Lord detests all the proud of heart. Be sure of this: They will not go unpunished. (Proverbs 16:5)

In our home, *hate* is one of those four-letter words we teach our kids to avoid. But in the case of pride, the word *hate* is an appropriate verb choice. In God's eyes, pride (the gross, me-obsessed kind, not the natural pride we feel over something good) is disgusting, detestable, and offensive — it's an abomination to the Lord.

In the New Testament, both Peter and James warn us of God's resolute response to the prideful: He will oppose them, always (James 4:6; 1 Peter 5:5). When you and I are prideful, we are literally setting ourselves up against the Lord.

The word *opposes* means "to resist, to arrange in battle against." God is so serious about pride that He will allow His army to go to battle against the proud. That's one scary truth worth taking to heart. Be warned: "Those who walk in pride He is able to humble" (Daniel 4:37b). There's no option B when it comes to pride. Pride and a swift downfall go hand-in-hand.

Ironically, this big-headed sin is simple to recognize in others, but a little trickier to recognize in ourselves. To help wake us up to our prideful ways, read the following *Pride Inventory*. Check each box that applies to you.

- ☐ When you listen to a sermon, do you instantly think of other people who would have benefited from hearing that message?
- ☐ When someone else is talking, do you have a hard time listening because you're already thinking about what you will say next?
- ☐ Are you defensive when someone corrects you?
- ☐ Do you have a hard time apologizing to certain people?
- ☐ Do you like to get the last word in so you can make sure your voice was heard?
- ☐ Do you get tired of having to repeatedly ask God for help?
- ☐ Do you interrupt others when they're speaking so you can share your thoughts?
- ☐ Do you have a hard time asking for help?
- ☐ Do you feel like you have to keep it all together all the time?
- ☐ Do you frequently correct or criticize people?

If you marked any (or all) of the boxes above, you're in good company. We all struggle with pride to some degree — it's part of our fallen nature. But we must fight it daily so we don't allow ourselves to become numb to our sin.

When we recognize pride rearing its ugly head in our lives, wisdom teaches us to humble ourselves — to intentionally lay ourselves down (James 4:10). Remember, we can either bend our knee to our sovereign Maker or He will bend it for us. The choice is ours.

GRAB YOUR FORK

Why do you think God hates pride so much?

Read through the *Pride Inventory* again. Where does pride reveal itself most in your life?

Most of us have blind spots in our lives regarding pride. If you're willing, ask someone you trust where you might be missing the sin of pride in your life. Instead of becoming defensive, thank them for their response and talk to the Lord about what they revealed.

PRAYER

Father God, open my eyes and soften my heart so that I can see my pride for what it really is. Tear down any walls I've built and/or any self-exalting platforms I've tried to establish apart from You. And thank You for Jesus, who forgives, restores, transforms, and makes whole. I humble myself before You today and trust in Your mighty hand to lift me up as I press on in my pursuit of becoming more like You.

HUNGRY FOR MORE?

Read Proverbs 18:12. Many biblical scholars believe pride is the root of all other sin. Do you agree with them? Why or why not? (It may help to list some of the sin you struggle with. Can each one be traced back to the sin of pride?)

Read Daniel 4:29–37. Answer the following questions:
What was Nebuchadnezzar's sin? (verse 30, 32)

How did God humble him?

What is one truth you will take away from this powerful story?

8
Keeping Pace Together

When pride comes, then comes disgrace,
but with humility comes wisdom.
Proverbs 11:2

As you read through the Book of Proverbs, you'll notice most of the book is written in couplets, or pairs of sentences, that relate to one another. Some couplets compare (show how two things are similar), some complete (reinforce the meaning), and some, like today's key verse, contrast (show how two things are different).

Today's verse contrasts pride and humility. It states that when pride strolls in (when we're consumed with self and walking apart from God), disgrace follows closely behind. The two — pride and disgrace (or shame) — keep pace together like traveling companions. Although in the moment the prideful might appear to be living on a high, as we learned yesterday, a fall is inevitable. Shame is coming.

Conversely, the humble are accompanied by wisdom. Like two peas in a pod, you won't find one without the other.

The dictionary defines *humility* as "a modest opinion or estimate of one's own importance." According to Charles Spurgeon, humility is "to make a right estimate of oneself." Humility isn't degrading ourselves. Instead, it's about maintaining a proper view of oneself in relation to God and others.

Humility is about remembering where we came from:

> The LORD God formed the man from the dust of the ground and breathed into his nostrils the breath of life, and the man became a living being. (Genesis 2:7)

Humility understands that it doesn't matter where we grew up or whether we graduated from a prestigious school with a fancy degree. It doesn't matter if we're short, tall, fast, slow, skinny, round, strong, or weak. You and I came from dust, and to dust we will return (Genesis 3:19). Humility knows that "without God we are nothing. Without His care, without His provision, without His love, we would still be dust."[2]

Wisdom accompanies the humble because the humble stay connected to the Source of wisdom Himself. If pride nods, "I don't need you on this one. Thanks, God." then humility throws out her arms and screams, "Stay close. I've got nothing without You!"

Or listen to how this rabbinic paraphrase puts it,

> "Lowly souls become full of wisdom as the low place becomes full of water."[3]

During Hurricane Harvey, when unprecedented waters fell on South Texas, I watched the news in disbelief as waters rose across miles and miles of the city I once called home. As I scrolled through pictures on Facebook, I couldn't help but notice that only the houses built on the few high points of our old neighborhood stayed dry. Every low place was covered by water.

Similarly, the humble are flooded with wisdom because their disposition fits them to receive and be filled by God. They remember that they came from dust. And what can dust do apart from the hands of its Maker?

GRAB YOUR FORK

C.S. Lewis says that true humility is not thinking less of ourselves, but thinking of ourselves less. How do you describe the difference?

What do you think it means to humble yourself (James 4:10)?

How can we practice making ourselves low before the Lord, knowing that He is the lifter of our heads?

Pride

PRAYER

Jesus, thank You for showing me the beauty, power, and strength of living with humility before God and man. Would You grow in me a proper view of self — careful to live in the tension of being a woman who is both made of dust and made in the image of God? Make me a ready vessel for Your wisdom, Lord. I want to show the world more of You.

HUNGRY FOR MORE?

Read Luke 18:9–14 slowly. Picture yourself in this parable. Who do you resemble most? Why?

Jesus is our perfect example and only way to humility. Read Philippians 2:1–11. List a few ways Jesus demonstrated humility.

What are some practical ways we can consider others better than ourselves?

9

Humble Rewards

The fear of the Lord teaches a man wisdom,
and humility comes before honor.
Proverbs 15:33

We don't have to read far into the pages of Scripture to notice that the kingdom of God operates under a different set of values than the kingdom of this world. In the world, success, status, power, and popularity rise to the top of the value system. It's the people with the loudest voice, the biggest following, the most money, and the largest platform who get the world's attention.

But God is attracted to something quite different. In the kingdom of God, the Lord notices those who put others first, who serve without recognition, and who, when called to do so, lay themselves down for the sake of another. In the kingdom of God, it's the humble who capture God's attention.

While the world crowns those who fight their way to the top and applauds the man who stands on the highest stage, God bends down low to hear the prayers of the meek (Psalm 116:2 NLT). He strengthens the weak (Isaiah 40:29), lives close to the lowly (Isaiah 57:15), and takes the side of the helpless (Psalm 116:6). God lifts and honors those who humbly place themselves under His sovereign hand (James 4:10).

Remember what we learned in Day 7:

> God opposes the proud but gives grace to the humble. (1 Peter 5:5)

If God's stance against the prideful looks like an army, swords drawn and ready for battle, then how do we picture His grace? Maybe it's like the powerful force of an undercurrent that takes us places we could never go alone, or an invisible bubble that surrounds us like an impenetrable shield. Or maybe it's a fresh breath of air that lifts us to higher ground — above the circumstances of our day-to-day.

The grace of God is the gift of His enough-ness. It's His acceptance that goes before us, His forgiveness that frees us, and His holiness

Pride

that shapes us to become more like Jesus. Grace is the Lord's unearned and undeserved favor — His presence, His power, His kindness, and His strength at our disposal. *This* is the incomparable gift for the humble.

To receive this gift, we practice humility over and over and over again. Like a muscle that expands with use, we repeatedly rehearse the exercise of submitting our hearts to Jesus. For me, practicing humility starts first thing every morning with the words, "I need You, Jesus," and then continues all throughout the day. We can practice this when we're feeling overwhelmed by our unmanageable to-do list, when we're blindsided by confrontation at work, and when we pick the one line in the grocery store that isn't moving. In these moments (and the hundreds of others just like them), we submit our heart to the Lord and trust in His grace. We exchange our lack, our need, our I-don't-have-it-in-me for His grace, His enough-ness, His let-Me-be-everything-you'll-ever-need.

From the world's perspective, the kingdom of God operates in ways that seem backward and upside down. It's a place where the back of the line is really the front, the great are ignored, and the overlooked are rewarded. For the first will be last and the last will be first (Luke 13:30), and he who humbles himself will be exalted (Luke 18:14).

GRAB YOUR FORK

What usually captures your attention first, the proud or the humble? Which is more attractive? Why?

Why do you think God goes to great lengths to bless the humble?

When is it most difficult for you to humble yourself?

PRAYER

Father God, thank You for your incomparable gift of grace. Thank You for seeing me in my weaknesses and need and promising to be enough for me. Continue to work the trait of humility into every part of my life. I trust that in this process of becoming, You will never give up on me.

HUNGRY FOR MORE?

According to Proverbs 22:4, what are some other blessings given to the humble?

Do you think there's a connection between fear of the Lord and humility? Why or why not?

Read Luke 14:1, 7–11. As you read Jesus' parable, pay attention to what in the story resonates with you. Do you remember either the elation of being considered more special than you thought you were or the deflation of being thought more ordinary? What do you think this says about your view of self?

When are you most tempted to grab the best for yourself?

In those circumstances, how can you practice putting others before yourself?

10
Stay Teachable

He who listens to a life-giving rebuke
will be at home among the wise.
He who ignores discipline despises himself,
but whoever heeds correction gains understanding.
Proverbs 15:31–32

To date, one of the most challenging (and by challenging, I mean annoying) seasons in parenting has been when one (or more) of my children suddenly thinks they know it all. It's happened to all three of them at different ages, but the symptoms of their know-it-all-ness have been marked by the same obvious words: *"I know."* Whether we're giving them advice or instruction or just stating the facts, when my kids start slinging these two words around on repeat, we know we've got a pride problem.

Repeatedly the Book of Proverbs warns us about the dangers of pride and counsels us to combat this ugly sin by staying teachable. Keep listening, it tells us. Pay attention. Don't stop learning ... for this is the way of the wise.

Proverbs 19:20 states this clearly:

> Listen to advice and accept instruction, and in the end you will be wise.

Maintaining a teachable spirit is one beautiful characteristic of humility that keeps our heart and mind open to becoming — it's how we continue to learn and grow. Being teachable involves:

1. Listening to advice.
2. Accepting instruction.
3. Heeding correction.

There have been times in my life when I was allergic to all three of those things. I wasn't interested in others' advice, didn't need their instruction, and felt above correction. Although I would never admit those things out loud, in my spirit I was an unteachable know-it-all.

Pride

Over the years, however, after walking through several humbling experiences, I've learned that there's no such thing as arriving, having all the answers, or having it all together. Now I understand this journey of becoming is an ongoing process of learning, unlearning, and relearning, if we stay teachable.

While recognizing my worth, I must also remember my limitations and neediness before the Lord. We all have something to learn as we navigate through this journey called life, everyone except God.

> We cannot wrap our minds around God's wisdom and knowledge! Its depths can never be measured! We cannot understand His judgments or explain the mysterious ways that He works! For, "Who can fathom the mind of the Lord? Or who can claim to be His advisor?"
> (Romans 11:33-34 THE VOICE)

Humility teaches us that we don't need to know everything if we know the One who does. So we lean in close, confess our need, and walk closely with Jesus, our good teacher and friend.

GRAB YOUR FORK

Do you know anyone with an unteachable spirit? What stands out most to you about this person?

Being teachable involves listening to advice, accepting instruction, and heeding correction. Which of these three are most challenging for you?

Have you invited anyone into your life with permission to advise, instruct, and correct you? If so, who? If not, why?

How do you want to improve to become more teachable (both in relationship to God and others)?

PRAYER

Heavenly Father, I pray today that You would expose any areas of my life where I've become unteachable. Reveal the high places where pride has hardened my heart and blinded me from my need for You. Don't let me get away with living like I know it all. Instead, soften my heart and make me teachable. I want to be a lifelong learner, ever becoming more like You.

HUNGRY FOR MORE?

Read the following verses. Write down what each teaches about the importance of leaning into the Father and His Word for teaching and instructions.

Psalm 25:4–5, 8–15

Isaiah 55:2–3, 8–9

2 Timothy 3:16–17

How can you put what you've read from these passages into practice today (and tomorrow, and the next day ...)?

WEEK TWO: *Recap and Reflection*

DAY 6

Pride is big-headed and conceited, but it's also disguised as the strong, independent woman.

DAY 7

God hates pride. It will not go unpunished.

DAY 8

Wisdom accompanies the humble because the humble know who they are (a child made in the image of God) and who they're not (God).

DAY 9

God gives the gift of His enough-ness (grace) to the humble.

DAY 10

Life is an ongoing process of learning, unlearning, and relearning. Stay teachable.

What did you learn about God this week?

How does this truth point you to Jesus?

[1]Anderson, Hannah. *Humble Roots: How Humility Grounds and Nourishes the Soul.* Chicago, IL: Moody Publishers, 2016, p. 71.

[2]*Ibid.*, p. 56.

[3]Barnes Notes on Proverbs 11, www.biblehub.com.

Words

The tongue has the power of life and death,
and those who love it will eat its fruit.
Proverbs 18:21

11

Life or Death

The tongue has the power of life and death,
and those who love it will eat its fruit.
Proverbs 18:21

Did you know the Book of Proverbs has more to say about our words than anything else in our lives? There's a good reason ... Studies show that on average, most of us say between 10,000 and 25,000 words each day. With so many words coming out of our mouths, it's understandable that God would put great importance on the words we speak.

Given the amount of them alone, our words matter. After all, what else do we do 20,000 times a day? But more than that, the Book of Proverbs teaches us that our words matter because of the incredible amount of power they carry.

Listen to how The Message translation puts our key verse for today:

> Words kill, words give life; they're either poison or fruit — you choose. (Proverbs 18:21 MSG)

Our words matter because they have the power of life and death. They can be used as a deadly weapon or a life-giving tool, both in our own lives *and* in the lives of others.

Think about how words have affected your family, marriage, parenting, friendships, church, and workplaces. Consider the impact of the tongue on your own and others' hopes, dreams, perspective, reputation, and identity. Both in positive and negative ways, the power of words has affected us all.

Sticks and stones may break my bones, and words *can* hurt, no matter what they say. I think most of us understand this. We know our words carry power. We just aren't always intentional about how we wield them.

Now let's think about the words we speak to and about *ourselves*. The truth is, you and I talk to ourselves all the time. Sometimes we talk to ourselves out loud, but most of the time that conversation takes place inside our heads. What about *those* words? Do you usually use life-giving words (encouraging, positive, hope-filled words) or words that kill (discouraging, negative, put-downs)?

As Proverbs 18:21 states, in one way or another, we will "eat the fruit," or bear the consequences, of our words. Many of the personal struggles I faced in my late 20s and early 30s were the result of unhealthy and unwise self-talk. Because most of the words I spoke about myself were negative, my insecurities were at an all-time high. But when I changed my words, my identity, security, and confidence changed too.

Changing my words didn't happen overnight. Over time, as I pressed deeper into the pages of my Bible, God opened my eyes to the many lies I believed about myself. During that season, I learned what it means to take captive every thought to make it obedient to Christ (2 Corinthians 10:5). We do this by holding our thoughts (about ourselves or anything else, for that matter) up to the light of God's truth. If our thoughts don't line up with the thoughts of the One who made us, we must intentionally choose to exchange those lies for His truth. When the words we speak to and about ourselves change, our lives will change too.

The words we speak matter. They either nourish (Proverbs 10:21) or destroy (Proverbs 11:9). They crush (Proverbs 15:4) or heal (Proverbs 16:24). We get to choose. How will you use your words today?

GRAB YOUR FORK

Spend some time considering the impact that words have had on you. What are some specific ways that the words of others have shaped the life you now live (positive and/or negative)?

53

Now consider the words you speak to and about yourself. What kind of words do you more often use?

☐ Words that kill

☐ Words that give life

Self-talk also includes the conversations we replay and/or rehearse in our minds. How do these "tapes" affect your daily life? Do you think they are helping or hindering you?

How can you change/improve the words you speak to yourself?

PRAYER

Father God, wake me up to both the careless and intentional ways I use words to hurt, manipulate, and tear down myself and those around me. Today and always, I want to speak words that build up, nourish, and heal. Grow in me the desire to speak words that give life, never words that kill. I can't do this without You, Jesus.

HUNGRY FOR MORE?

Read James 3:3–8. According to this passage, what are the dangers of the untamable tongue?

Read Proverbs 10:11. While it's easy to see how words can spread like a wildfire, scorching everyone in its path, it's also important to recognize the positive ways our words can spread. I can think of several people in my life whose words to me are a life-giving fountain. These people encourage me with truth and honesty.

They lift me up and inspire me toward bigger faith and a greater dependence on Jesus. My life wouldn't be the same without them.

Who in your life is a life-giving fountain? _____

Specifically, how does this person lift up, encourage, and inspire you?

Consider sending him or her a quick text today saying "thank you" for the powerful impact his or her words have had on your life. Or better yet, go the old-fashioned route and send a handwritten note of thanks in the mail.

Read Proverbs 12:18. Spend a few minutes talking to Jesus about the hurtful words and lies that have been spoken into you. Let Him sit with you in your pain and tend to those wounds.

Now talk to the Lord about the words you speak to yourself. Surrender any self-talk wounds to Him. As you practice taking your thoughts captive (2 Corinthians 10:5), ask Him to redeem the words you speak to yourself.

Finally, when you're ready, ask Him to reveal the ways your words have pierced others, especially those in your home. If necessary, apologize for the careless, cutting words you've spoken, and ask for forgiveness.

12

Overflow

A wise man's heart guides his mouth,
and his lips promote instruction.
Proverbs 16:23

Personally, I've had a difficult time moving on from Day 11's material. As I typed out the words on the pages you just read, the gravity of them weighed heavily on me. I care deeply about honoring the Lord with my mouth. And I want to speak life, not death, to the people around me. Not coincidentally, however, in the process of writing, I got into a war of words with a friend and said some hurtful things to her. Before our conversation ended, I felt the remorse of my sin and even some shame. Although I apologized, I couldn't take my words, or the sting of them, away. How can I be writing about words and mess up so profoundly?

As I prayed about it through tears, the Lord quietly reminded me that He doesn't reveal sin or weakness to mock or condemn, but to heal and change me, if I let Him. Maybe, like me, you need to recognize the ways you've misused your words, then receive the forgiveness that is yours in Jesus. When Jesus died for our sins, He died for all of them, even the mean words we've said. So, agree with Him that you messed up, and start again. Remember, every day we begin again. The Lord's mercies are new every morning. Great is His faithfulness (Lamentations 3:22–23)!

Now, considering what we learned yesterday, how can we be assured of producing good words that can feed, lift up, and bless others?

Today's key verse teaches us that our heart guides (instructs, teaches) the mouth. If we want to be intentional about the words that flow from our mouths, we must trace our words all the way back to their place of origin, the heart.

Listen to how Jesus puts it:

> The good man brings good things out of the good stored up in his heart, and the evil man brings evil things out of the evil

stored up in his heart. For out of the overflow of his heart his mouth speaks. (Luke 6:45)

The truth of Jesus' words mirrors that of the proverb. Jesus *is* living Wisdom. He knows that our words expose the state of our heart. They give us away, spilling over to reveal to ourselves and others what's really going on inside. Try as we may, we can't clean up our words without first allowing the Lord to tend to our heart.

Have you ever been surprised by the words spewing from your mouth? I have. Anytime we catch ourselves speaking unkindly, gossiping, or bursting out in anger at our family, we need to check our heart. Sometimes it's not the specific words but the tone or attitude of our delivery that's revealing a heart issue. In either case, a heart inspection is necessary. What sin or darkness have we stored inside, and why? How can we release them?

We'll close today with two vulnerable prayers from David. I borrow these words often when my own words expose me. Maybe you'll want to borrow them, too.

> Search me, O God, and know my heart; test me and know my anxious thoughts. See if there is any offensive way in me, and lead me in the way everlasting. (Psalm 139:23–24)

> May the words of my mouth and the meditation of my heart be pleasing in your sight, O LORD, my Rock and my Redeemer. (Psalm 19:14)

GRAB YOUR FORK

On a scale of 1 to 10, how often do you pay attention to the words you speak?

Have you ever tried to manage your words without giving much thought to the state of your heart? How did that work out for you?

Is it comforting or disconcerting to you that God intimately knows every detail of your heart (based on Psalm 139:23–24)?

PRAYER

Father God, I invite Your searching gaze into my heart. Examine me through and through; find out everything that may be hidden within me. Lead me to the path that brings me back to You. May the words of my mouth and all the thoughts of my heart be pleasing in Your sight, O Lord, my Rock and my Redeemer.

HUNGRY FOR MORE?

Read Matthew 12:33–37 and James 3:9–12. Compare the main message of these passages.

What do you think accounts for any discrepancies you might see between them?

In what way will we be held accountable for our words?

13

Lies

The LORD detests lying lips,
but he delights in men who are truthful.
Proverbs 12:22

Oddly, I can only remember being punished once as a child. It's not that I was a perfect child (trust me!), but for some reason this one event is the only one seared in my memory. The incident happened over a piece of gum. I wanted more than one piece, but my mom said no. When I took the second piece anyway, I quietly hid its trash in my closet to get rid of the evidence. When my parents questioned me about it later, I lied. You can probably guess how this story ends. It turns out that my secret trash hiding place wasn't so secretive after all.

While this story is seemingly innocent, I'm sure we can all share a story or two about lying. It's one sin that's plagued us all. There has never been nor will there ever be anyone, apart from Jesus, who has never told a lie. Whether it's bold-faced or a little white lie, we've all missed the mark when it comes to honest words.

Our key verse for today is as straightforward as they come. The Lord is disgusted by lies. But what's so bad about lying? Why does the Bible use such strong language about dishonesty?

The Lord hates lying because all dishonesty is in direct contrast and opposition to His character. Not only will God never lie, but it's impossible for Him to do so. He is incapable of speaking anything less than perfect truth (Numbers 23:19).

But there's more. God hates dishonesty because lying is the defining characteristic of the devil (John 8:44). It's Satan's nature *and* his work to deceive. In Genesis 3, we read the story of the very first lie ever recorded in the Bible. Satan, disguised as a crafty serpent, lied to Eve about God's goodness and intentions in the Garden of Eden, and he's been lying ever since. Deception is the devil's primary weapon against God's children.

We can conclude, then, that when dishonest words flow from our mouths, we look more like Satan than Jesus. The thought of that makes my stomach turn. It's a sobering truth. But let's not get stuck here. We do have hope.

Whereas lies are characteristic of Satan, truth is characteristic of Jesus (John 14:6). As followers of Jesus, you and I abide (remain, stay) in truth. And as we continue to grow and be transformed into His likeness with ever-increasing glory (2 Corinthians 3:18), truth will invade our hearts and permeate every corner of our lives.

> But still, You long to enthrone truth throughout my being; in unseen places deep within me, You show me wisdom. (Psalm 51:6 THE VOICE)

In beautiful and mysterious ways, the Holy Spirit, the Spirit of Truth, works His truth into the fabric of our lives from the inside out (John 14:17). The more we saturate our mind and heart in His truth, the more it will find its way in us, filling us up and bubbling over in the words we speak. This is the Lord's desire for us all.

Although it's not always easy, telling the truth is always the wise thing to do. Learning to speak truth in love not only honors God, but it also mirrors His character. It's another way we can show the world more of Jesus.

> Oh Lord, keep our tongues from evil and our lips from speaking lies, we pray (Psalm 34:13).

GRAB YOUR FORK

How do you feel when you know you've been lied to? Why?

When is it the hardest for you to tell the truth?

Are there any areas or circumstances in your life where you've given yourself permission to lie or excused away lying?

Do you think there's such a thing as a good lie? Why or why not?

How does knowing that all lies originate in the devil affect/ influence your desire to speak truth always?

PRAYER

Father God, forgive me for lying. Thank You for the beautiful and mysterious ways the Holy Spirit works His truth into the fabric of my life from the inside out. Would You set a guard over my mouth, Lord? Keep my tongue from evil and my lips from speaking lies. In this journey of becoming, I want the words I speak to reflect more and more of You.

HUNGRY FOR MORE?

Read Proverbs 12:19. Which stands the test of time, truth or lies? What can you then infer about the chances of a lie staying hidden?

Read John 17:17. As believers, what is our standard and measure for truth?

Give an example of how you've seen or experienced the sanctifying power of God's Truth at work. (Sanctify means to cleanse, set apart, make holy.)

14
Like Cheap Candy

The words of a gossip are like choice morsels;
they go down to a man's inmost parts.
Proverbs 18:8

Let's begin today with a definition. A *gossip* is "a person who habitually reveals personal or sensational facts about others, rumor or report of an intimate nature." Most of us are well acquainted with this noun and familiar with its corresponding verb. There's a good chance we've even been this person a time or two.

Sadly, gossip has become so commonplace that we don't even recognize its conversational hold on us. Gossip fills pages of magazines and occupies the headlines of much of our entertainment "news." It's whispered by the workroom copy machine, spoken on the sidelines of our kid's last sporting event, and disguised as a prayer request in between church pews. When we hear it, we can't help but lean in. And if we're honest, we like it best when it's juicy and painfully delicious to swallow down.

Read THE VOICE translation of our key verse for today:

> Whispered gossip is like a delicious first course: it is devoured *with pleasure* and penetrates deeply. (Proverbs 18:8 THE VOICE)

The Message version of this verse likens gossip to eating cheap candy — it's easy to share and easy going down, but in the end it makes us sick. I know all about this kind of sickness because cheap, sweet candy happens to be my favorite weakness. Without even thinking, I can down handfuls of sugary-goodness at a time. My binging only stops when my stomach turns over to raise its white flag.

In the Bible, gossip is often used interchangeably with *slander*, another word worth defining. Slander is "the utterance of false charges or misrepresentations which defame and damage another's reputation, a false and defamatory oral statement about a person."

Gossip and her sister, slander, are addictive and destructive habits. They're both fruit of a foolish, undisciplined, and unrestrained mouth. These unattractive sins of the mouth destroy reputations, ruin friendships, and hurt everyone involved. We know this, yet still we get drawn in. Don't we?

Practically speaking, how do we radically remove gossip from our lives?

> There is more hope for a fool than for someone who speaks without thinking. (Proverbs 29:20 NLT)

Our all-out attack against gossip is waged with careful and intentional speech. We must think before we speak! The more we become deliberate with our words, intentional about speaking life, not death, the less gossip will flow from our mouths.

Now let's make this practical for our everyday lives. If the key to less gossip is thinking before we speak, what specific things would be helpful to think about?

Here are some questions to think through before we open our mouths to share with others:

- *Is this my story to tell?*
- *Does this conversation shed a negative or unflattering light on anyone?*
- *What's my motivation in sharing this? Is it to feel superior, to get attention, to feel like part of the group, because I'm angry or envious or bored, or something else?*
- *Will my words make this conversation more loving, more grace-filled, or more encouraging?*

Imagine the difference in our conversations if we took these questions seriously. What if we all just chose one of the above questions to serve as our filter before we speak? Could one intentional pause before we speak really impact the quality and impact of our words?

Our words matter. They affect lives, reputations, friendships, and our own well-being. It's time to rid ourselves of gossip for good.

GRAB YOUR FORK

When it comes to gossip, which are you more tempted by, sharing gossip or participating by listening?

Why do you think gossip is so enticing to us?

Today's challenge: Pick one of the questions above to be your filter before you speak. Write it down and commit to putting it into practice to help rid your speech of gossip.

PRAYER

Father, forgive me for all the times I've participated in gossip, both as the speaker and the listener. By Your Spirit, please convict my heart about the ways I engage in gossip, and give me courage to stop any harmful or destructive speech among my peers. I desire to speak only words that encourage and lift up those around me.

HUNGRY FOR MORE?

Read the following verses from Proverbs. Note what each says about gossip/slander.

Proverbs 10:18

Proverbs 11:13

Proverbs 16:28

Proverbs 20:19

Write Ephesians 4:29 in the space below. How can this verse be used as a filter to rid gossip from our lives for good?

15

Hold Your Tongue

When words are many, sin is not absent,
but he who holds his tongue is wise.
Proverbs 10:19

When I look back through the devotions this week, I'm suddenly compelled to jump online and search for a human muzzle. Solomon took the words right out of my mouth ...

When words are many, sin is not absent ...

It's inevitable; the more I talk, the more I'm capable of blabbing my way into sin. But the proverb doesn't end there.

... but he who holds his tongue is wise. (Proverbs 10:19)

When it comes to words, wisdom is found in speaking with restraint *and* simply speaking less. The wise measure their words. They don't spout out every thought that pops into their head. Their words are deliberate. Their silence is thoughtful.

While Proverbs 10:19 tells us to *hold* our tongue, Proverbs 13:3 puts it this way:

He who guards his lips guards his life, but he who speaks rashly will come to ruin.

We guard our lips by limiting our speech. We don't allow every thought, opinion, and/or response to fly out of our mouths without thinking about them first. In doing this, we protect our lives from sin and heartache, and we protect others from our lazy speech. Remember in Day 12 when we talked about speaking words we can't take back?

When is it most difficult for you to *hold* or *guard* your tongue? When you or someone you love is personally offended? When someone is annoying you? When you know you're right? I could add many more examples to that list (like when the referee at your child's soccer game isn't doing his job), but I'll stop there. It's no easy task to tame our tongue, restless evil that it is (James 3:8).

The good news is, we don't walk the way of wisdom alone. Again, I'm challenged to turn my heart back to this truth: Wisdom is found in a relationship with Jesus. You and I don't need a muzzle to hold our tongues, and we don't have to carry a roll of duct tape in our purses either. Instead, we only need to turn to Jesus, who delights in living His wise and graceful life in and through us.

Out of necessity and often desperation, we breathe silent prayers all throughout the day. And we practice daily, hourly — every minute when necessary — the submission of our mouths to Jesus, who is the Guard of our mouth and Holder of our tongue. He is our only way to becoming a woman who speaks with wisdom.

GRAB YOUR FORK

My life accurately mirrors the truth of Proverbs 10:19. What about you? When was the last time you ran your mouth straight into sin?

Conversely, describe a time when in wisdom you chose to hold your tongue.

When is it most difficult for you to hold your tongue?

Why do you think there is wisdom in speaking less?

In what ways could you practice speaking less?

PRAYER

Jesus, set a guard over my mouth, and keep watch over the door of my lips (Psalm 141:3). I want to represent You well with every single word I speak.

HUNGRY FOR MORE?

According to Proverbs 17:27–28, what is one quick way to improve your reputation?

Read James 1:19–26. This section of Scripture could be titled: "Less Talk, More Action." List three to five things that stick out to you from this passage.

Why do you think James considers a controlled tongue a good test for one's spirituality? Do you agree or disagree? Why?

WEEK THREE: *Recap and Reflection*

DAY 11

Words have the power of life and death. We choose how we use them.

DAY 12

Words flow from and expose what's in our heart.

DAY 13

God hates lying and esteems honesty.

DAY 14

Gossip is an addictive and destructive habit. It's the product of an undisciplined and unrestrained mouth.

DAY 15

When it comes to words, wisdom is found in speaking with restraint and simply speaking less.

What did you learn about God this week?

How does this truth point you to Jesus?

Emotions

Above all else, guard your heart,
for it is the wellspring of life.
Proverbs 4:23

16

Guard Your Heart

Above all else, guard your heart,
for it is the wellspring of life.
Proverbs 4:23

Emotions are tricky, aren't they? And confusing. One minute we're up, and the next we're down. I don't know about you, but sometimes my emotions feel like a real-life roller coaster I don't want to ride.

This week we're going to look to the Book of Proverbs to help us figure out what to do with all these up-and-down emotions. After doing some research, I learned that the word *emotion* isn't found anywhere in the Bible. Like with other biblical concepts (such as the Trinity), we can't approach this topic as a word study. However, we can certainly open the pages of Scripture to learn how to handle the full gamut of our emotions. The Bible was written by *feeling* men about a *feeling* God to a *feeling* audience. None of us are robots. Especially not God.

In the Old Testament, we read of a compassionate God who is moved by His children. We see His fierce love to set apart, defend, and protect, but we can't miss His righteous anger, too. In the New Testament, Jesus shows us the heart of our feeling God by the tender way He lived. Through His life we see compassion, love, amazement, and joy but also grief, anger, sorrow, and distress (just to name a few).

Because we are made in the image of God, we have the power to feel, too (Genesis 1:27). And like our words, our emotions flow from our heart. Although not always reliable, they are the indicators, or reporters, of what's going on inside us.

Our key verse for today gives us important wisdom regarding our heart, the seating place of all our emotions. Specifically, it commands us to *guard* it.

We often hear this verse quoted to young girls falling in love for the first time. Guard your heart, we tell them. Protect yourself from love and heartbreak. But I'm not sure that's the best understanding of this verse.

The biblical meaning of the word *heart* is "the inner man, which includes the mind, will, heart, and understanding." That's why Proverbs 4:23 names our heart "the wellspring of life," or the place from which everything flows. Some translations go so far as to say our heart determines the course of our life.

The Hebrew word *guard* in this verse is translated as "keep, watch over, preserve." We are commanded to keep watch over and preserve the condition of our heart because it's the place from which everything flows — all our thoughts, words, emotions, and actions.

Like a watchman set high on a tower keeping watch over a city at night, you and I are called to watch over and guard our heart, paying close attention to what goes in *and* what comes out.

WHAT GOES IN

The first part of guarding our heart involves keeping watch over what we allow into our heart. Guarding our heart does not mean protecting ourselves from love and connection. Instead, it means we set up a guard against lies, deception, temptations, and distractions of the heart. We want to protect our hearts from anything that could defile, contaminate, tempt, or lead us astray. We also want to watch out for things that lull us to sleep, make us complacent, or draw us away from our first love, Jesus (consider the things we read, watch, and scroll through on social media).

WHAT COMES OUT

The second part of guarding our heart involves keeping watch over what flows out of our hearts. This is where our emotions come in. Guarding our heart does not mean we put our heart and all our feelings on lockdown. Instead, we let our emotions operate under their God-given role as *reporter* versus *boss*. As reporters, our emotions are intended to gather information and inform. They help us understand and make sense of what's going on in our topsy-turvy hearts.

We will talk about this much more in the days ahead, but for today let's practice guarding our heart by paying attention to what's going in and what's coming out of our heart. How are these things influencing/affecting the current state of your heart?

GRAB YOUR FORK

When you close your eyes and picture God, what expression is on His face? Is He happy, sad, mad, or indifferent? What emotion best defines your view of God?

How did today's conversation about guarding your heart differ from how you've viewed it in the past?

Which, if any, do you pay attention to more often: what's going into your heart or what's coming out? Why do you think both are important when it comes to guarding our heart?

PRAYER

Heavenly Father, thank You for giving me the power and ability to feel. Although I don't always understand my emotions, I know they are a gift from You. Please teach me how to guard my heart — the place from which all of life flows. I want to be more intentional and discerning about what I allow in and more aware of what comes out so that I can become more like You.

HUNGRY FOR MORE?

Read Proverbs 4:20–27, which includes today's key verse. What are some practical ways to guard your heart, according to this passage?

Read Psalm 119:36–37. What role does God's Word play in guarding our heart?

17
Trust

Trust in the LORD with all your heart and lean not on your own understanding; in all your ways acknowledge him, and he will make your paths straight.
Proverbs 3:5–6

"Follow your heart" is a popular mantra of our world today. When big decisions surface and we don't know what to do, "follow your heart" seems like wise advice. It sounds simple, hopeful, and liberating ... that is, until we understand the true nature of our heart.

> The heart is deceitful above all things and beyond cure. Who can understand it? (Jeremiah 17:9)

The prophet Jeremiah teaches that *above all things*, our hearts are deceptive. While they are the "wellspring of life," they also can't be trusted or understood. The heart wants what it wants, and many times it wants the wrong things.

These hearts of ours are prone to wander; they get caught up in the temporary and are often sidetracked by lesser loves. And because they're naturally bent toward sin, they can easily mislead our emotions. To trust our heart makes us a thickheaded fool (Proverbs 28:26 AMP).

So what are we to do with these hearts of ours? Our key verse for today gives us our answer. You and I must learn to trust God with our heart and with everything that flows from it, too. Only the Lord can see, know, and understand the inner workings of our heart. Only He can search and know us better than we know ourselves (Jeremiah 17:10; Psalm 139:1–4).

As we explored in Day 16, our emotions are given to us by God to be indicators of the heart. They are meant to inform us. Trouble comes, however, when we trust our emotions and allow them to act as a boss instead of a reporter.

Here's what it looks like when our emotions become our **BOSS**:

1. Experience a very real emotion to a situation.

2. Feel the emotion and trust that it's telling us the truth without examination.

3. React out of that emotion.

Now here's what it looks like when our emotions are **REPORTERS**:

1. Experience a very real emotion to a situation.

2. Feel the emotion but pause to hold that emotion before the Lord.

3. Submit your reaction to Him, trusting that He will lead and guide you.

4. Respond appropriately in wisdom.

Here's an example of what this could look like in our day-to-day life using a real-life scenario from mine.

Every morning I join the many moms who drop off their middle schooler at the front of the school. As I drive into the parking lot, I pull my car to the back of the slow but moving drop-off line. About halfway through the long line, we come to a standstill. Looking around the cars, I notice several drivers have decided to park themselves right in front of the school to wait for the bell to ring instead of obeying the carpool-line rules of drop-and-go. After sitting still for a minute or two, my emotions begin to flare. I feel frustration, annoyance, and indignation rising to the surface. Now at this point, I have two options. I can:

#1: Listen to and trust my unexamined feelings (Those parents are selfish. They don't respect other people's time and obviously think the world revolves around them), then react by honking my horn and/or pulling my car up next to the rule breakers to yell at them for not moving their cars. Or ...

#2: I can turn my feelings over to Jesus, take a deep breath, recognize that I too have broken the drop-off rules in the past, extend grace, turn up the music, and sing with my daughter while we attempt to wait patiently.

The result of the situation is radically different when our feelings act as a boss instead of a reporter. I'd like to say I've reacted like #2 every time, but the truth is, I've been both. At times I've driven off peacefully, while other times I've pulled away feeling (and looking) like a fool.

Trusting our feelings then reacting out of every fleeting emotion isn't living in wisdom. It's dangerous and foolish. But God is greater than our hearts, and He's greater than our feelings too (1 John 3:20).

I understand that the realities of life aren't lived out in a neat and tidy four-step process. However, when we break this process down to simple steps, we begin to recognize that the defining moment of every situation comes down to trust.

Who are we going to trust? A heart that must be guarded and a roller coaster of emotions, or our unchanging God (Malachi 3:6)?

GRAB YOUR FORK

In your own words, describe how emotions benefit us when they operate as a reporter.

Now describe the dangers of emotions operating as our boss.

As you go about your day, make a list of all the emotions you experience. Next to each, write what preceded that emotion, then your response to the felt emotion. What does your response tell you about the object of your trust? Is it the Lord or your own heart?

PRAYER

Father God, I pray that You would give me faith to trust You with my whole heart, as well as the many emotions that flow out of me, too. Although I know I can't always trust or even understand my emotions, I can trust You, Jesus, for You are greater than my heart. Give me wisdom to turn to You in all my feelings rather than following every whim of my heart. I place my hope and all my expectations in You.

HUNGRY FOR MORE?

Read Proverbs 3:5-8. Think about what it would look like for you to trust God with every emotion. Which of the following do you think would result from choosing to trust God over your feelings? (Check all that apply.)

☐ I would talk to God more throughout the day.

☐ I would desire to be in the Word more so I could know and follow His ways.

☐ I would talk less and listen more.

☐ I would feel more at peace.

☐ Other _____

Read Ezekiel 36:25-27. How does this passage demonstrate that God is greater than our hearts (1 John 3:20)?

18
Hold Me Back!

A fool gives full vent to his anger,
but a wise man keeps himself under control.
Proverbs 29:11

Several years ago, this proverb occupied the center stage of our home. Of all traits that I hoped to pass down to my children, a short fuse wasn't one of them. But there we were, with a child clearly struggling with his temper, and a mom who couldn't dole out consequences without first looking in the mirror. In my best teacher handwriting, I wrote the words of this verse on white paper in thick sharpie and taped it to the refrigerator door. And as a family, we recited the words, acknowledged our feelings, and practiced holding back — especially when we were tempted to blow.

When it comes to our emotions, the way to wisdom is found in using restraint — in learning to keep ourselves under control. This doesn't mean we're supposed to turn off or deny our feelings. Feelings are meant to be felt. However, restraint is one way we learn to guard our heart and trust in the Lord over our feelings.

At first glance, the idea of holding back or restraining ourselves seems like a personal fight — after all, it is called self-control. But again, it's important to redirect my independent flesh back to the truth that I'm never called to walk this road alone. Wisdom is found in a relationship with Jesus.

When our emotions flare and we're tempted to fly off the handle, we can't trust our feelings and follow our heart. That's the way of the fool. Instead, in wisdom, we learn to lean on Jesus, who promises to meet every one of our needs perfectly.

Remember that four-step process we discussed yesterday?

1. Experience a very real emotion to a situation.
2. Feel the emotion but pause to hold that emotion before the Lord.

Emotions

3. Submit your reaction to Him, trusting that He will lead and guide you.

4. Respond appropriately in wisdom.

Restraint happens in steps two and three, when we choose to pause (hold back) and submit (lay down) our emotions to Jesus.

Interestingly, the Hebrew word used in Proverbs 29:11 for "keeps himself under control" is the same word used for "still" in Psalm 89:9.

> You rule over the surging sea; when its waves mount up, you still them. (Psalm 89:9)

Isn't that what our emotions feel like at times — a raging sea? How many times have we allowed violent emotional waves to rise and crash down, taking out everything and everyone in their path? That's what happens when we trust solely in our feelings — when we allow them to be the boss and dictate our next move.

In times like these when I feel the waves mounting, it helps me to remember that God still rules over the surging seas. The wind and waters of our soul are at His command, too, if we will trust in Him.

GRAB YOUR FORK

Think back to the last time you were driven by your emotions in a situation and as a result reacted poorly. What could it have looked like (both internally and externally) if you had shown restraint by turning to Jesus instead of your emotions?

How is pausing to turn to Jesus different from relying on willpower and self-control?

81

PRAYER

Jesus, I don't want to live as a slave to my bossy emotions. Instead, I want to learn to turn to and submit to You — the God who rules over the wind and waves of my soul. I trust You, Jesus, to be the guard and guide of my heart, no matter what life throws my way. Teach me how to walk each day with You.

HUNGRY FOR MORE?

Read Mark 4:35–41. Write down Jesus' command to the waves in verse 39.

I have so many questions as I read this passage of Scripture. I wonder how long it took for the disciples to turn to Jesus in that furious storm. How long had they been thrown around and battered by the waves? How much water was in the boat already? How close were they to going under? And why did they wait to call to Him? Hadn't they already seen His miracles and experienced His power? Didn't they know who was with them?

Jesus said, "Peace! Be still!" ... and in an instant, all was calm again.

Where in your life do you need to hear Jesus' words, "Peace! Be still!" right now? (What thoughts, emotions, and/or circumstances?) Will you lean in and trust Him today?

19
Turning Away Anger

Mockers stir up a city,
but wise men turn away anger.
Proverbs 29:8

Of the many emotions we feel, anger is the most powerful of them all. In the Bible, there are several Hebrew words used for our English word *anger*, but interestingly many of them are defined more by what they look and sound like than what they are. Anger is "a breath of the nostrils, snuffing, and snorting." It's also loud, screaming voices, the slamming of doors, and a steady stream of tears. Anger feels hot-faced and shaky, like a fuse that's lit and ready to blow.

At its best, anger is merely another emotion intended to inform us of what's going on inside. At its worst, anger is a powerful and unruly boss. Most of the time, anger barks unreasonable demands, impairs our judgment, and severely limits our perspective. When left unchecked, it can lead to a host of other unhealthy, sinful behaviors such as hate, rage, wrath, unkindness, unforgiveness, bitterness, slander, and jealousy, just to name a few. To be clear, the feeling of anger isn't sinful. It's what we do in response to anger that causes us to go astray.

Across the board, the Book of Proverbs describes the fool as one who acts out in anger. These people are the easily annoyed, the quick tempered, the reckless, and the hotheads (Proverbs 12:16; 14:16–17, 29). These verses describe those who allow the emotion of anger to boss them around and dictate their next move. Raise your hand if you've been that woman. I know ... I've been her, too. We all experience the emotion of anger. And unfortunately, when we let it hold us hostage, it marks us as a fool.

Anger labels you a fool. (Ecclesiastes 7:9b NLT)

So what are we to do with this powerful emotion when it surfaces? According to the proverbs, while the foolish react, a wise woman learns to turn away from or diffuse her anger.

Obviously, this is easier said than done. Most of the time, when anger boils to the surface in my life, I feel entitled to my feelings *and* my spontaneous reaction to them — justified even. But when, in obedience, I choose to pause, take a breath, give it some time, and turn my heart to the Lord (instead of immediately reacting in anger), I give Jesus room to show me a more graceful way to respond, one marked with love, patience, and extra measures of self-control.

Turning away anger takes practice. Like with every habit, it takes intentionally choosing to replace an old behavior with something new. But it also takes resolve. If we believe that God's Word is true and His ways are better, then we'll be convinced (before a situation even arises) that anger will never serve us well. And no matter how justified we may feel, we'll willfully choose to humble ourselves and lay our feelings at the feet of Jesus. It is in that place that we can grow and become wiser.

GRAB YOUR FORK

Do you consider yourself someone who is quick to anger? Why or why not?

Pay attention to what triggers your anger. List a few things that often set you off. If you're feeling particularly brave, ask someone you trust what triggers they see in your life (without defending yourself), and write them here.

Anger is always a response to threat. If anger is an indicator of something happening inside of us, what could anger be pointing to (pride, fear, lack of perceived control, etc.)?

PRAYER

Heavenly Father, I don't particularly like that Your Word labels me a fool when I give vent to my anger. However, when I sit in Your presence and consider Your character, I understand why it's true. You, my God, are righteous and just in all Your ways. I am not, especially when it comes to reacting in anger. So today I choose to submit to and trust in You. Thank You for Your Word and the truth that sets me free.

HUNGRY FOR MORE?

According to Proverbs 15:1, 18 and 19:11, what are some practical ways we can turn away from anger?

Read Psalm 37:1–11. What does this passage say to do with anger?

How does trusting God play into our ability to turn away from anger?

Read Ephesians 4:22–27. How do you think anger is associated with our "old self"?

How does anger "give the devil a foothold"? How can going to bed angry give the devil this opportunity?

20

Choose Joy

An evil man is snared by his own sin,
but a righteous one can sing and be glad.
Proverbs 29:6

Often throughout the day we feel emotions we don't want to feel. Doesn't it seem like disappointment, frustration, and sadness hit us at the most inconvenient times? (*Why am I crying right now?*) We can't control the emotions we feel, no matter how hard we try. In a way, they choose us. However, there is one emotion we can choose (indirectly, at least). That emotion is joy.

In case you were wondering, "choose joy" is nowhere to be found in the Bible. Don't bother Googling it. I've already tried. Joy isn't a commodity that we can purchase off a shelf, and it's not an emotion we can pick off a feeling chart when we're having a rotten day.

Instead, joy is a gift we're given when we choose to walk each day with Jesus — when we learn to abide in His presence and trust in His "with-ness" to sustain us. It's the fruit of a life tethered wholeheartedly to Jesus (Psalm 16:11).

When we read today's key verse, we see the evidence of a joyful life — a woman who is free to sing and be glad. The "righteous ones" this verse speaks of are those who have entrusted their lives to Jesus. Their consciences are clear and their hearts are at peace, not because they are without sin, but because they choose to rest in the forgiveness and peace of Jesus. If you're a follower of Jesus and didn't recognize yourself as one of the "righteous ones," now is the time to start claiming your true identity. The "righteous one" is you!

Joy can and should flow from our lives, as women who belong to Jesus, no matter what our circumstance. Because we have the Holy Spirit living and breathing inside us, we can experience joy, an emotion much deeper and more enduring than happiness.

Happiness is "the state of well-being and contentment." It's a feeling that comes and goes depending upon our good circumstances. Joy, however, cannot be manipulated by the rise and fall of our day.

I love Kay Warren's definition of joy: "Joy is the settled assurance that God is in control of all the details of my life, the quiet confidence that ultimately everything is going to be alright, and the determined choice to praise God in every situation."[1]

I've not only felt this emotion, but I've seen it, too. I saw it on the brave face of my friend Amy as she awaited yet another round of energy-draining chemo. I witnessed its strength in my friend Allison, who smiled through tears as she worshipped at her husband's funeral. I heard its resolve in the voice of my friend Kara, when she stood among her older sisters and gracefully recited her mom's eulogy. The joy of the Lord is our strength — it's what keeps our heads up and our knees from buckling as we fight the good fight of faith on this side of eternity.

But joy is also available and ours for the taking during our day-to-day normalcy, too. It's in the worship songs that play in our head as we drag ourselves to the grocery store one more time before dinner. It's in our pleasure as we hear that our teenager has listened to our instruction and turned down offers to drink at a party. It's in our determination to keep showing up to serve in our thankless role as a volunteer or our challenging job. And it's in our kindness as we climb out of bed one more time to meet the needs of a sick child.

Joy is rooted in the choice to trust God's faithfulness and goodness, no matter what the circumstance. It's the work of the Holy Spirit that springs from a heart that leans its full weight on God (Galatians 5:22–23).

The Bible teaches us that the joy of the Lord is our strength (Nehemiah 8:10). Joy is a defining characteristic that sets us apart from the rest of the world. It allows us to grieve differently, struggle differently, hope differently, and live differently than those living apart from the gospel. Joy is one way we can show the lost the face of Jesus.

Whether positive or negative, our emotions play an important part in our everyday lives. And though they can sometimes feel like a roller coaster ride we didn't sign up for, every emotion is a gift from God. The power to feel is a gift. Whether it's a positive emotion (such as joy, peace, gratefulness, and hope) or ones we view as negative (such as sadness, loneliness, discouragement, or regret), all emotions have the potential to teach us about ourselves and draw us closer to God, if we let them.

GRAB YOUR FORK

In your own words, describe the difference between joy and happiness.

Who are a few people in your life that exude joy?

To what do you attribute the overwhelming overflow of this emotion in their lives?

PRAYER

Father God, thank You for allowing me to experience the beautiful, life-giving emotion of joy. No matter what life throws my way, by Your Spirit, help me to choose joy by leaning on and trusting in You. May the joy that others see in me be a defining characteristic that draws them closer to You.

HUNGRY FOR MORE?

Read Nehemiah 8:10. Describe a time when you've seen or experienced the reality of "the joy of the Lord is your strength."

Read Romans 15:13. List some of the fruit of our lives when we trust in Jesus.

Read James 1:2–4. We don't have to be happy when we face trials, but why does James tell us we should choose to be joyful in them?

WEEK FOUR: *Recap and Reflection*

DAY 16
We guard our heart by being intentional about what goes in and aware of what comes out of our heart.

DAY 17
Because our hearts are deceptive, we are instructed to trust God with our heart instead of trusting in and reacting to every fleeting emotion.

DAY 18
Wisdom is found in using restraint and turning to Jesus in our emotions.

DAY 19
Anger labels us a fool. Wisdom teaches us to turn away from anger.

DAY 20
Joy can and should flow from our lives as followers of Jesus, no matter what the circumstance.

What did you learn about God this week?

How does this truth point you to Jesus?

[1]Kay Warren, *Choose Joy: Because Happiness Isn't Enough.* Grand Rapids, MI: Revel, 2013.

Relationships

He who walks with the wise grows wise,
but a companion of fools suffers harm.
Proverbs 13:20

21
Walk with the Wise

He who walks with the wise grows wise,
but a companion of fools suffers harm.
Proverbs 13:20

Have you ever heard the saying, "Show me your friends and I'll show you your future"? Or what about this one: "You are the company you keep"? These sayings aren't just pithy statements about the importance of the friends we choose. They're actually rich in spiritual truth.

This week, as we turn our eyes to becoming wise in our relationships, our key verse for today gives us wisdom we can apply to every relationship we pursue.

> Become wise by walking with the wise; hang out with fools and watch your life fall to pieces. (Proverbs 13:20 MSG)

To some extent, most of us have already lived out the reality of this truth, haven't we? We've seen and/or experienced firsthand how getting involved with the wrong crowd can send us down paths we never dreamed of taking. We also understand the value of one faithful friend who's willing to grab our hand and walk with us along the straight and narrow (Matthew 7:13–14).

The word *walk* in our key verse refers to the people we do life with. These are the friends we spend the most time with. They're the ones we don't have to clean our house for, who have seen us before makeup and coffee, and who know the ins and outs of our daily life. As we discussed in Week 1, the wise are those who fear God and live their lives out of their relationship with Him. They love the Word of God and seek to honor and obey the Lord in all they say and do.

Today's proverb teaches us that if we surround ourselves with wise friends, we will grow in wisdom, too. Conversely, if we attach ourselves to foolish friends (those who live apart from God and the truth of His Word), we will ultimately hurt ourselves.

Relationships

Do not be misled: "Bad company corrupts good character." (1 Corinthians 15:33)

In a very literal way, our friends rub off on us. So, what kinds of marks are your friends leaving on you? Do you spend most of your time with friends who talk poorly about their husbands, gossip about their neighbors, and whine and complain about everything under the sun? Or do you surround yourself with friends who esteem their families, encourage one another, and try to seek out the good in life? The character of our friends will shape and influence our lives, one way or another.

I've seen this principle play out clearly in the lives of my children. While there are times I recognize the influence of their friends for the better, it seems like the negative traits and behaviors are stickier. My kids often come home mirroring their peers' weaknesses rather than their strengths. If this principle is true and obvious in them, it's undoubtedly apparent in me, too.

Wisdom, then, teaches us to separate ourselves from foolish friends. Separating from them doesn't mean we abandon them. It's important to continue to love them, pour into their lives, and pray for them, but we don't have to walk with them anymore — we don't have to give them a lot of time. You and I are never called to sacrifice our character or our relationship with the Lord for the sake of another person.

In every season of life, our friendships are instrumental to our transformation and growth as we become the woman God created us to be. It's critical, therefore, that we choose wisely.

GRAB YOUR FORK

Think back to the friendships you had growing up. How did those relationships influence the decisions you made and ultimately the path you took in life (both for the positive and the negative)?

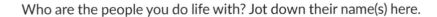

Who are the people you do life with? Jot down their name(s) here.

Based on the biblical definition, are these relationships marked by wisdom? Why or why not?

In what ways do you think you are rubbing off on your friends?

PRAYER

Father God, please give me wisdom and discernment in choosing those whom I do life with because I understand that those who walk with the wise grow wise, but a companion of fools suffers harm. Open my eyes to the ways my friends are rubbing off on me. I desire to invest my time in relationships that encourage me toward more of You.

HUNGRY FOR MORE?

Read 2 Corinthians 6:14–18. The metaphor of a yoke is used frequently in the Bible. A yoke is "a wooden crosspiece that is fastened over the necks of two animals and attached to the plow or cart that they are to pull." The purpose of a yoke is to connect two animals together so they can share the weight of a heavy load and more efficiently and effectively plow a field.

How does the metaphor of being unequally yoked relate to the relationships we pursue (such as our friendships, our significant other, and the mentor/role models we choose)?

How can a believer be a friend and witness to an unbeliever without becoming yoked to them?

22
Together

As iron sharpens iron,
so one man sharpens another.
Proverbs 27:17

I'd never heard the word *people* used as an adjective until I met my friend Blake. After I mentioned to her that my family was planning to attend a popular community event over the weekend, she replied, "Oh, I can't go to that. It's way too people-y." I laughed when she said it and instantly knew what she meant. To my introverted friend, some situations are just too people-y.

The Bible teaches us, however, that people-y or not, we must learn to relate wisely with all the people. Today's key verse gives us a glimpse of why.

When two iron blades are rubbed together, they both become sharper and more effective for use. Their dull surfaces shine again, like brand new. And so it is when we learn to live in close proximity to one another. When we live in community, with our lives rubbing up against the lives of others, we become sharper and more effective for use.

No man was created to live as an island. Just as God exists in eternal community (as God the Father, God the Son, and God the Holy Spirit), He created us to live and thrive in community, too.

Let me be the first to say that living in community isn't easy. There have been times when I was ready to throw in the towel on the whole idea of purposefully living with others. I was happy to lock myself up with my people and call it good. But the Lord wouldn't let me stay there.

> Let us not give up meeting together, as some are in the habit of doing ... (Hebrews 10:25a)

In community, we must choose to keep showing up, keep peeling back layers, and keep pressing in, even when it gets uncomfortable. Although we are sure to get rubbed in ways that cause friction, the

Relationships

discomfort can be worth it. I've learned firsthand how much I need people in my life who are willing to ask questions that challenge me, who encourage me with truth, and who live their lives in ways that inspire me toward more of Jesus.

Living in community isn't life-giving because it's comfortable or easy. Instead, it stretches and challenges us in the process of continually becoming. Without it, we are hard pressed to learn and grow.

Do you live in community with others like this? If you do, lean into these relationships, and handle them with care. If you don't, pray for it. Often, we don't have because we don't ask (James 4:2). But either way, remember there's no companion better than Jesus.

> A man of many companions may come to ruin, but there is a friend who sticks closer than a brother. (Proverbs 18:24)

In a plot twist like no other, Jesus, the Savior of the world, demonstrated His love by laying down His life for us, the ones He calls His friends (John 15:12–17). Not only is He everything we're looking for, but in Him is everything we need. Jesus listens and counsels, protects and abundantly provides. He is our faithful companion until the end.

GRAB YOUR FORK

We find community in many different places (such as our neighborhoods, schools, workplaces, family members, churches, etc.). List some of the places you specifically find community.

Which of these communities inspire you toward more of Jesus? How do they sharpen you?

In what ways are you avoiding or hiding from the community God has given you? Why?

PRAYER

Jesus, thank You for not only coming to be my Savior but also promising to walk with me as a friend. Remind me in little ways throughout the day of Your companionship — I want so badly to grow in my everyday walk and dependence on You. Thank You also for the people that You have placed in my life. Please open my eyes to the community You have provided all around me, and give me the courage to lean into those relationships so we all can become more like You.

HUNGRY FOR MORE?

Read the following verses. For both passages, note why it's important to keep showing up in the places we have community.

Hebrews 10:24–25

Ecclesiastes 4:9–12

Read 1 Corinthians 12:12–27. How does this passage make you feel about your importance in the body of Christ?

23

Authority

Fear the LORD and the king, my son,
and do not join with the rebellious,
for those two will send sudden destruction upon them,
and who knows what calamities they can bring?
Proverbs 24:21–22

Especially in today's culture, which operates under the philosophy that "respect is earned, not freely given," it's important to know what God's Word says about how we are to relate to those in positions of authority.

Today's proverb states it plainly: We are to fear (honor, respect, and submit to) the Lord first, then the king (or in our case, those appointed in authority over us). It says nothing about those in authority needing to prove themselves to earn our respect. As it is in the military, we are called to honor and respect the rank or position, even if the person is hard to respect.

> Every person must submit to and support the authorities over him. For there can be no authority in the universe except by God's appointment, which means that every authority that exists has been instituted by God. (Romans 13:1 TPT)

This passage teaches us that only God can grant positions of authority. Because of this, it's our duty to honor and respect the position God has given them, whether we personally like and/or agree with them, or not. This teaching is tough because it removes our assumed right to act as judge, measuring and weighing others' character, actions, and values against our own.

> To honor the Lord, you must respect and defer to the authority of every human institution, whether it be the highest ruler or the governors he puts in place to punish lawbreakers and to praise those who do what's right.
> (1 Peter 2:13–14 TPT)

When we respect and submit to our authorities, we are respecting and submitting to the Lord, who has seen fit to put those people in their ordained place of authority. As Christians, we are called to a higher standard than that of our world. It's not our right to decide which authority in our lives deserves our respect. When we disrespect those in positions of authority, we are disrespecting God and living in opposition to His Word.

There may be times when someone in authority asks us to do something contrary to God's Word. In those situations, we are expected to obey God and follow His commands first and foremost, even if that means going against our authority. However, even in these situations, we are expected to do it in a respectful manner.

In big and small ways, we show respect (or a lack of it) every day in our actions and words. Consider the following scenarios and how situations like these play out in your life:

- You give your child permission to ignore his teacher's instructions because you don't agree with her rules.

- You read a post on social media about an elected official that makes your blood boil. You comment harshly, making sure your opinion is heard, and share your own two cents about it on your own page, too.

- You're frustrated that your athletic super-star sat on the bench for part of the big game, so you give the coach the cold shoulder after the game and bad-mouth him in the car on the way home.

- You constantly criticize the president and attack his leadership, regardless of your political party.

- You're furious (and embarrassed) for getting pulled over for speeding, so you're rude to the police officer when he gives you a ticket.

- You talk negatively about your boss at home and undermine his authority in the office.

Again, this teaching from God's Word is tough. In situations like these, what message do our words/actions communicate to those around us about how to treat the authority figures in their lives?

Fear the Lord; honor your authorities. This is the way of the wise.

GRAB YOUR FORK

Who are the authority figures in your life? (List at least five.)

When it is most difficult to respect those in authority over you?

Relationships

PRAYER

Father God, thank You for the leaders that You have sovereignly placed in my life. Forgive me for the ways I have disrespected and undermined them, both in my actions and words. I understand today that promotion and authority only come from You. Soften my heart and give me the wisdom and grace to better honor them, and in doing so, better honor You. Especially when I disagree with them, help me trust You and Your ways above my own.

HUNGRY FOR MORE?

Read the following passages. After you read them carefully, write one truth that sticks out to you that is counter-cultural to our world today.

1 Peter 2:13–17

Hebrews 13:17

Romans 13:1–7

What is one change you'd like to make in response to these truths?

24

Drip, Drip, Drip

Better to live on a corner of the roof
than share a house with a quarrelsome wife.
Proverbs 25:24

Have you ever noticed that the Bible often repeats itself? As in any piece of literature, repetition is used for emphasis to help the reader better understand the importance of the author's intended message. In the Bible, repetition is often used to draw our attention to important truths targeted specifically at our weaknesses (where the enemy is especially at work).

Today's key verse is a perfect example. Five times in the Book of Proverbs, the writer warns his son to steer clear from the "quarrelsome wife." While the warning of this proverb is directed to a man (Watch out for this kind of woman!), we would be wise to heed his warning, too (Don't become this kind of woman!).

> A quarrelsome wife is like a constant dripping on a rainy day; restraining her is like restraining the wind or grasping oil with the hand. (Proverbs 27:15–16)

Two of the five proverbs that reference the quarrelsome woman liken her to a constant dripping on a rainy day. Try to picture the scene with me. It's been pouring rain all night, and you wake up to a large puddle of water in your family room. Obviously, your roof has a leak. Quickly you soak up the water with towels and grab a large bucket to catch the steady trickle of water. "Drip, drip, drip." At first, you're satisfied and relieved by your temporary solution. But after some time, the constant dripping becomes maddening. You want to escape the noise, but where can you go?

Ladies, is this us? Have our words becoming exhausting (even maddening) to those within earshot of us, like constant dripping on a rainy day?

A quarrelsome woman is habitually ill-tempered — she criticizes, nags, bickers, argues, and complains. She's rarely content and makes everyone around her uneasy. While I think it's safe to say that none of us aspires to these traits, sometimes they describe us. When comfort sets in and life happens, who are we behind closed doors?

Because of Solomon's repetitious warning, not to mention my own weakness in this area, I don't want to miss the caution of becoming this kind of woman. Yes, having a quarrelsome spirit is detrimental to our marriages, but it hinders all our other relationships, too.

Do we have our friends and family walking on eggshells, careful not to stir us up or say the wrong thing to set us off? Do we harp on other people's faults, dredging up the past, pointing out their failures and disappointments — constantly wearing them down? Do we have people whispering around us, "Be careful! She's in one of her moods"?

In times like this, when God's Word feels like a mirror reflecting parts of ourselves that we'd like to keep hidden, it helps to remember that God isn't finished with us yet. In our lifelong pursuit of becoming, as women walking and growing with Jesus, we want to become more teachable, more grace-filled, and more aware of and sensitive to our weaknesses and shortcomings — not hardened and/or ignorant to them. God wants this for us, too.

So today let's heed the proverb's warning: Don't be a quarrelsome woman. Every time you catch yourself nagging or complaining about or to someone, immediately turn to Jesus and pray for them. When we make the decision to turn to and connect with God in moments of weakness, He will work in our heart and change our behavior — for our good and to His glory. Amen?

GRAB YOUR FORK

Sometimes, even when we think we're helping, our words only come across as nagging. What do you think is the difference between being helpful and nagging?

When are you most tempted to nag, bicker, or complain?

Relationships

In times like the ones you identified, what feelings and emotions proceed your quarrelsome words or attitude (for example, fear, pride, or lack of control)?

PRAYER

Heavenly Father, I don't want to be like the quarrelsome woman in the Book of Proverbs who wears people down — like a constant dripping on a rainy day. I'm so grateful that You're not finished working on me yet. I pray today that You would create in me a new habit that prays for others when I'm tempted to whine, nag, or complain. Use these moments of weakness to display Your strength, Jesus. I want less of me and more of You.

HUNGRY FOR MORE?

If you struggle with nagging, complaining, and arguing, how can leaning in to Philippians 2:14 encourage and challenge you to only speak words that give life to those around you?

Read Proverbs 12:4 and Proverbs 31:10–12. If you're married, in what ways can you practice bringing good and not harm to your husband (in word and deed). If you're not married, you can apply the same question to the people you do life with regularly. How can you bring them good and not harm?

Read Proverbs 14:1. Does this verse relate to the quarrelsome woman? If so, how?

25
Train a Child

Train a child in the way he should go,
and when he is old he will not turn from it.
Proverbs 22:6

Today's key verse is one of the most quoted verses in the Book of Proverbs regarding parenting. Therefore, we'll begin today by first digging into this proverb from a parenting perspective. However, if you don't have children, hang with me. Before we close, we'll talk about the potential impact this verse could have on future generations when applied to every relationship we have with those younger than us.

The Hebrew word translated as *train* in Proverbs 22:6 is defined as "train up, dedicate, initiate." In this proverb, we learn one of our primary roles as a parent is to dedicate and train up our children to know and love Jesus.

When our children were little, my husband and I stood before our local church and pledged to raise them up and train them according to "the Way." That dedication ceremony was an important moment for us. However, if that one day was the only investment we made in dedicating our children to Jesus, we've missed the mark as parents. It is our responsibility daily and repeatedly to equip, train, and show them the way to a thriving relationship with Jesus.

The most profound way you and I can influence our children toward Jesus is for us to live our own lives personally dedicated to Him. Our kids learn more from what they see than what they hear. If we want our kids to grow up with an authentic faith and genuine passion for Christ, then we need to model it. They need to see it in us first.

We can show them what it looks like to believe in a great, big God by letting them see us step out in bold faith. We can show them that God's Word is essential and relevant by not only reading the Word but also doing what it says. We can show them the beauty of the forgiveness and grace of Jesus by letting them see us mess up and asking for forgiveness. We can show them our dependence on Jesus by letting them hear us pray. If in parenting more is caught than taught, what message is our life teaching them?

There's a second application of this verse that I'd like for us to consider. If you have more than one child (and probably even if you don't), you know there's no one-size-fits-all approach to parenting. When it comes to direction, communication, discipline, and even understanding, there's a good chance that what works for one child probably won't work for another.

When Proverbs 22:6 tells us to train our child "in the way he or she should go," it's talking about parenting to that child's unique bent. A child's bent is their God-given personality, temperament, character, interests, and abilities. This includes knowing what makes your child smile, what breaks their heart, and what makes them light up with interest, passion, and desire. Knowing these things about our kids won't happen by accident. Instead, as parents we invest in becoming students of our children by paying attention.

When we know each child's unique bent, we can better know how to wisely train, guide, and encourage them to become the people God created them to be. You and I have the unique opportunity to know these children living under our roof better than anyone else. It's our privilege and responsibility to cheer them on as they discover and live out their God-given purpose in life.

And finally, as much as we'd like this proverb to be a promise to claim, there's no stamp of guarantee for us to hold on to. Even the best parents can't make their children follow Jesus. Our responsibility in parenting is to teach, model, and encourage. It's our children's responsibility to choose it for themselves.

I've heard it often said, "It takes a village to raise a child." And when it comes to our faith, I believe that saying is true, too. It takes a village. The more the world turns away from the Lord, the more the body of Christ (which includes all of us) needs to step up to invest in and raise up the next generation to know and love Jesus. Each of us has a responsibility to those who come behind us to train them in the way they should go, so when they are old they will not turn from it.

Again, we do this by investing in the kids around us, not just our own offspring — whether that's a class full of kids in Sunday school; the teenagers in your local youth group; the friends of your children who show up at your house, ride in your car, and play on the same sports teams; your nieces, nephews, and grandkids; your friends' kids; and the ones who run up and down your street.

This doesn't mean we always need to be armed and ready with an on-the-spot Bible lesson. We simply need to be willing to slow down and pay attention to the kids around us so that we can see, call out, and encourage the very best in them. When we're willing to pour ourselves into the lives of the kids God has already sovereignly placed around us, we participate in passing the baton of faith to the next generation.

GRAB YOUR FORK

Whether you are a parent or not, write down the names of the younger people in your life whom you (could) have an influence on.

Think ahead with me. When these kids grow up and set out to live on their own in this big, wild world, what do you want them to take with them spiritually? (Is it a love for God's Word, a heart to serve, passionate worship, bold faith, a rich, thriving prayer life? What else?)

How are you authentically modeling these things in your own life, as opposed to merely talking about them?

Relationships

WEEK FIVE

Have you pinpointed your child's unique bent? Ask the Lord to give you eyes to see your child as He does, not as you want them to be.

PRAYER

Jesus, thank You for the children You have placed in my life. I thank You that You have perfectly and uniquely crafted each one of them to know and follow You. Please give me eyes to see them as You do, not as I want them to be, so that I can see, call out, and encourage the very best in them. Instill in me the desire to invest in the next generation to love and serve You.

HUNGRY FOR MORE?

Read Proverbs 4:1–13. As a refresher, who is the author of most of the proverbs, including this one?

Who were his parents? (2 Samuel 12:24)

What part did his parents play in his spiritual upbringing? (Proverbs 4:3–4, 10–11)

Read Hebrews 13:7. Think about people in your life who have invested in your faith throughout the years. How can you pay forward the investment that was made in you? If this is something lacking from your childhood, what can you do now to begin that legacy of faith?

Recap and Reflection

DAY 21

If we surround ourselves with wise friends, we will grow in wisdom, too. Conversely, if we attach ourselves to foolish friends, we only hurt ourselves.

DAY 22

When we live in community, we become sharper and more effective for use.

DAY 23

We are called to respect and submit to the authorities that the Lord has sovereignly placed over us out of submission to Him.

DAY 24

A woman with a quarrelsome spirit is wearing on everyone she encounters. Don't become this kind of woman.

DAY 25

Our primary obligation to younger generations is to dedicate and train them up to know and love Jesus.

What did you learn about God this week?

How does this truth point you to Jesus?

Identity

Charm is deceptive, and beauty is fleeting;
but a woman who fears the Lord is to be praised.
Proverbs 31:30

26

Beauty

Charm is deceptive, and beauty is fleeting;
but a woman who fears the LORD is to be praised.
Proverbs 31:30

This week, as we close out our time together, we're going to focus on identity. Specifically, I'd like to uncover a few places where we're prone to put our trust (or rely/depend on) rather than the Lord. No other topic has more influence on becoming than our identity. Therefore, we'll begin our discussion with beauty or outward appearance.

Today's proverb comes at the end of a long passage written by a king passing down his mother's words of wisdom to his own son. In the passage, he describes what he calls "a wife of noble character," but to most of us, she's better known as the *Proverbs 31 woman*.

Growing up in the church, I've always viewed the Proverbs 31 woman as the pinnacle of true womanhood. If there was ever an "it girl," this woman was it. Not only was she a woman of strong character and sound wisdom, but she was also highly skilled, resourceful, and compassionate to all around her. Interestingly, however, the passage says nothing about her physical outward appearance. We hear nothing about her youthful glow, toned figure, or ageless beauty.

This fact should make us pause.

If you were asked to describe an "it girl" today, how much weight would you give to her physical appearance? If the magazine covers that dominate shelf space in the grocery store checkout line could speak (and I think they're actually shouting loud and clear), they'd tell us a woman's beauty is key to her achievement and success. Image is *everything*. But how much of what we see today is an accurate picture of reality? You and I are bombarded daily by pictures that are airbrushed and edited to perfection. Let's face it — most of us will never look like those cover girls on the magazines, or at least not the edited versions being sold to us. Plus, historically, there's no consistent definition of physical beauty. The measure and standard is constantly changing, leaving us chasing one trend after another.

So again, it seems that we're caught in the cross fire between the message of the world and God's Word.

> Charm can be misleading, and beauty is vain and so quickly fades, but this virtuous woman lives in the wonder, awe, and fear of the Lord. She will be praised throughout eternity. (Proverbs 31:30 TPT)

If charm and beauty are only deceptive forms of vanity, does this mean we should shatter all our mirrors and do away with all attempts at personal care? The easy answer is no. After all, our bodies are a temple, the sacred residence of the Holy Spirit. As stewards of these earthly tents of flesh, we are called to honor and glorify God with our bodies (1 Corinthians 6:19–20).

In this pursuit of continually becoming, we want to become more beautiful with each passing year, but we can't rely on our outward appearance for that. There aren't enough filters on Instagram to hide the reality of our fading beauty.

Instead, in wisdom, we recognize that it's our inward beauty, the unfading beauty of the soul, that deserves our focus and attention. While we're free to work out, highlight, wax, and pluck, it's useless to put our trust in an earthly tent that won't last. Because in the end, it's the woman who fears the Lord that will be praised.

GRAB YOUR FORK

Where do you invest more of your time, energy, and focus? Is it in the condition of your complexion, waistline, and wardrobe, or the state of your heart?

What are some ways you can invest in your inward beauty?

What changes can you make today to make the things you listed above a priority?

PRAYER

Father God, every time I look in the mirror, please remind me that You never look at me like the world does. While man looks at outward appearances, You see my heart (1 Samuel 16:7). Please give me eyes to see myself as You do, and give me the discipline it takes to invest in the condition of my heart rather than only on the condition of my complexion, waistline, or wardrobe.

HUNGRY FOR MORE?

One of my favorite beauty tips is found in Psalm 34:5. Do you know anyone who resembles the truth of this verse?

Read 2 Corinthians 3:18 and 4:16. Although outward beauty never lasts forever, what hope do we have in Jesus?

Read 1 Peter 3:4–5. There was a time when I resisted this verse because I felt light years away from being *quiet* or *gentle*. But in studying, I learned that the adjectives quiet and gentle aren't meant to describe our personalities. Instead they speak to our spirit and describe a person who is peaceful and at rest from the inside out. How can the attribute of a quiet and gentle spirit become our strength (see Isaiah 30:15)?

27
The Almighty Dollar

Whoever trusts in his riches will fall,
but the righteous will thrive like a green leaf.
Proverbs 11:28

The Book of Proverbs has much to say on the topic of money — much more than we can possibly cover in a week (let alone one day). So today we're going to zoom in on one central word from our key verse as it pertains to money: trust.

Let's read our key verse again, this time from the Amplified version:

> He who leans on *and* trusts in *and* is confident in his riches will fall, but the righteous [who trust in God's provision] will flourish like a *green* leaf. (Proverbs 11:28 AMP)

This proverb contrasts two people — the one who trusts in money and the one who trusts in God (called "the righteous"). And I've got to tell you, I'm not very happy about the fact that I can't be both.

I bet you weren't expecting me to say that, were you? While I'd *like* to say my hope is in Jesus alone, the truth is I also hope in a monthly paycheck that gets the bills paid and the children fed.

In the flesh, I rationalize my affection for money with talk of responsibility. The Bible has plenty to say about the importance of the hard-earned dollar, conscientious investing, and future saving, but I can't hide behind the façade of responsibility. At the heart of the matter, it always comes down to trust. Does our hope — our confidence, our security — rest in the Lord or in the amount of money in our bank account?

Because as today's proverb warns us: If we trust in money, we *will* fall.

Here's why:

#1: MONEY DOESN'T SATISFY

Listen to what Solomon, the wisest (and the richest) man in the world, says about money:

Whoever loves money never has money enough; whoever loves wealth is never satisfied with his income. This too is meaningless. (Ecclesiastes 5:10)

Notice the repetition of the word *love* in this verse. Although in many churches money has gotten a bad rap, it's not money that's the problem. It's the love of money that trips us up (1 Timothy 6:10). It has been said, "Money makes a lousy lover. The more you love it, the less it satisfies. The more you focus on it, the less it delivers." In the culture of the American Dream, it's easy to get caught up in the ever-revolving hamster wheel of just a little more. However, often we fail to realize that just a little bit more is never enough.

#2: MONEY IS HERE TODAY, GONE TOMORROW

Money might make us feel secure, in control, and important, but it isn't a stable rock to stand upon.

> Do not wear yourself out to get rich; have the wisdom to show restraint. Cast but a glance at riches, and they are gone, for they will surely sprout wings and fly off to the sky like an eagle. (Proverbs 23:4–5)

Trusting in finances is like building a sandcastle at the foot of the sea. With one crashing wave, everything you've built can come crashing down. Riches never last forever (Proverbs 27:24).

In contrast, the "righteous" referenced in the second part of our key verse, Proverbs 11:28, are the ones who trust in the Lord. They understand that provision comes from God alone. He's the One who both establishes our work (Psalm 90:17) and provides for our every need (Psalm 23:1). The righteous are "like a tree planted by steams of water, which yields its fruit in season and whose leaf does not wither. Whatever he does prospers" (Psalm 1:3).

Again, the issue with money isn't about the dollar or how much of it we have. Whether we're living paycheck to paycheck or have plenty stashed away for a rainy day, it always comes down to trust. What (or who) are we ultimately relying on: Almighty God or the almighty dollar?

GRAB YOUR FORK

Think through the following: Do you spend more time thinking about your finances or the Lord? Do you worry about your future more than you trust God with it? Is your posture toward money more like a clenched fist or a wide-open hand?

What do your answers to these questions indicate about the object of your trust?

In what ways have you experienced or seen proof that money doesn't satisfy?

PRAYER

Father God, open my eyes and expose the ways money has enslaved me. I want to learn to live with hands wide open, leaning on You as my sole Provider. Teach me how to steward my finances wisely. I put my trust, my hope, my confidence in You.

HUNGRY FOR MORE?

Read 1 Timothy 6:17–19. What are the commands for the "rich" in this passage?

Read Matthew 6:19–21. What do you think it means to "store up for yourselves treasures in heaven"?

What is the connection between our treasures and our heart? How is this true in your life?

Jeremiah 17:7–8 is a beautiful description of what it looks like to thrive like a green leaf (from our key verse). List some of the benefits of trusting in the Lord alone.

28

Fear of Man

Fear of man will prove to be a snare,
but whoever trusts in the Lord is kept safe.
Proverbs 29:25

During our first week together, we learned what it means to fear the Lord, but what does it mean to *fear man*? For starters, it's important to note that the Hebrew word used for *fear* in Proverbs 29:25 is different from the word used when talking about the fear of the Lord. The definition for *fear* in this verse is "fear, anxiety, trembling, anxious care." It says nothing about honor, reverence, or awe.

What the Bible calls *fear of man* is what we commonly think of as *people pleasing*. It's referring to those of us who are addicted to approval and preoccupied with the need to be liked and accepted.

Proverbs 29:25 warns us that when we're overly concerned with what others think about us, we walk ourselves into a dangerous trap. Read how The Message translation puts it:

> The fear of human opinion disables; trusting in God protects you from that. (Proverbs 29:25 MSG)

The opposite of the fear of man is trusting in the Lord. People who are filled with the fear of man have taken their eyes off the Lord. As the apostle Paul teaches, we can't fear man and trust God at the same time. It's impossible.

> Do you think I care about the approval of men or about the approval of God? Do you think I am on a mission to please people? If I am still *spinning my wheels* trying to please men, then there is no way I can be a servant of the Anointed One, *the Liberating King*. (Galatians 1:10 THE VOICE)

I know well what it feels like to spin my wheels trying to please others in hopes of winning their affection. It's exhausting. People pleasing is an empty well. It's a form of bondage that enslaves us.

Because ultimately, we serve what we fear.

After a big heartbreak in college (and the fear of rejection that closely followed), I became ensnared by the fear of man. It's safe to say I've struggled more with people pleasing as an adult than I ever did as a child. But as I've leaned into Jesus, He's woken me up to two important truths.

First, there's a big difference between loving people and pleasing them. Real love is others-centered. It's about elevating and esteeming them. Conversely, when we're seeking to please, the motive is usually selfish. We please others so we can be liked and accepted. It's more about protecting self (and avoiding rejection) rather than truly loving. I want to be one who loves others well, not simply one who seeks to please.

And second, there's also a difference between living *for approval* and living from the place of *already approved*. When we place our faith in Jesus, we rest as ones who are fully approved by God. The more settled we become in our identity in Christ, trusting in His character to define us more than our aching flesh, the more satisfied we'll become in His enough-ness. And in turn, the less we'll demand from others. I want to live my life from a place of settled confidence in my relationship with Jesus rather than looking for others to fill my seemingly bottomless cup. Don't you?

The fear of man is a trap, and let's face it, most of us are too difficult to please anyway. But God … He's compassionate and gracious — slow to anger and abounding in love and faithfulness (Psalm 103:8). He's the only One worth living to please.

GRAB YOUR FORK

Have you ever experienced the disabling feeling of people pleasing? If so, how has the fear of man affected you?

Why do you think we can't fear man and fear God at the same time?

PRAYER

Father God, remove from me the burden of people pleasing, and instead teach me how to love others well. Create in me the desire and discipline to seek You and be filled by Your love and acceptance instead of looking for love in all the wrong places. I need You, Jesus. And I love You. You are enough for me.

HUNGRY FOR MORE?

Read Mark 1:32–39. Jesus wasn't a people pleaser. Instead, what was the driving motivation behind all He said and did?

How can that same motivation keep you from the snare of people pleasing?

Read 1 Thessalonians 2:4. Paul lived to please God, not out of obligation (or to receive His approval) but out of love. What are some ways we can please God? (See Romans 12:1; Hebrews 11:6; and Psalm 147:10–11 for some ideas.)

29
Whatever You Do

*Commit to the L*ORD *whatever you do,*
and your plans will succeed.
Proverbs 16:3

When asked to tell a little bit about yourself, what do you usually say? Do you immediately begin with a list of all the things you do? Do you speak about your work, the many hats you wear, and the roles you play in this thing called life? For many of us, our work has taken over our identity, and when this happens — when our value and worth rest in *what we do* rather than *who we are* — our faith can become misplaced.

Today's key verse gives us the wisdom we need to keep work (and our faith) in its proper place. Our focus for this proverb is on the word *commit*. In the original language, commit means "to roll, to transfer what is rolled away from oneself to another." So in this case, we are called to roll whatever we do (our work) to the Lord.

For better understanding, let's read Proverbs 16:3 again, this time in multiple translations.

> Before you do anything, put your trust totally in God and not in yourself. Then every plan you make will succeed. (TPT)

> Put God in charge of your work, then what you've planned will take place. (MSG)

> Whatever you do, do it as service to Him, and He will guarantee your success. (THE VOICE)

From these translations, we can see three ways of viewing the word *commit* as they relate to our work.

#1: TRUST IN GOD, NOT YOURSELF

How much thought do you give to God when you work? Do you lean on Him regularly? Do you depend on His strength, His guidance, and His grace as you go about your day?

I love that the word *commit* in the original language creates a picture in my mind of rolling a ball. When it comes to trusting God and not in myself, it seems like no matter how many times I roll my way to the Lord, the ball keeps finding its way back into my lap. That's why our faith must be active. Like a game of hot potato, every time we feel its weight in our hands, we can learn to roll our work back to God's capable hands.

#2: PUT GOD IN CHARGE

I'm not going to lie — I like being in charge. This confession won't surprise anyone who knows me well. Based on every personality test I've ever completed, I'm hardwired to lead. It's taken some living and learning, however, to understand that being a leader and being in charge are two very different things.

When it comes to our work, whether that means running a Fortune 500 company, a class of fifth graders, or a family of five, wisdom teaches us to put God in charge. This frees us to release the reins and let God be the One who carries the burden and responsibility of control.

#3: DO YOUR WORK AS A SERVICE TO HIM

I will never forget a little conversation I had with God one day while doing the laundry. On this particular day, I was home alone and in a sour mood. After listening to the dryer ring its *I'm all dry* bell for the hundredth time, I grabbed the large pile of laundry and threw it on my bed. As I began sorting and piling, I rattled off complaints in my head, "I'm so tired of doing this *stupid* laundry. It's all I ever do. These people need to learn to do some things for themselves. I don't know why I'm still doing their laundry for them." And then came another little voice, soft but authoritative, gentle but firm (and yes, still in my head), "But will you do it for *Me*?" Cue tears.

> Whatever you do, work at it with all your heart, as working for the Lord, not for men, since you know that you will receive an inheritance from the Lord as a reward. It is the Lord Christ you are serving. (Colossians 3:23–24)

Yes, whatever we do — whether it's emails and spreadsheets or laundry and floors. When we do our work in service to Jesus, everything has purpose, value, and reward.

GRAB YOUR FORK

Define or describe your work.

What would it mean to trust in God and not yourself in your work?

What would it look like (and feel like) for you to put God in charge at work?

PRAYER

Lord, today I choose to put my confidence and dependence in You for every aspect of my life, including my work. Teach me how to commit all my doing to You. I trust You. I want You to be in charge. Teach me, day by day, to work as though I'm serving You, not men.

HUNGRY FOR MORE?

Read Psalm 37:3-6. Make a chart of this passage. On the left side, write down what we are commanded to do. On the right side, write the reward (or what God will do).

Read Colossians 3:17. What do you think it means to "do it all in the name of the Lord Jesus"?

Here's how I process this verse. If I can't attach the words "in the name of the Lord Jesus" to the end of whatever I say or do, then I probably need to make a change.

Here are some examples:

- I can't yell at my kids in the name of Jesus ... but I can discipline them with patience in the name of Jesus.

- I can't talk about my friend behind her back in the name of Jesus ... but I can hold my tongue from gossip in the name of Jesus.

- I can't complain about the house being a mess in the name of Jesus ... but I can serve my family by cleaning the house in the name of Jesus.

Does that help? Let's practice living out the meaning of Colossians 3:17 today.

30
Faith that Grows

Pay attention and listen to the sayings of the wise;
apply your heart to what I teach, for it is pleasing when you keep
them in your heart and have all of them ready on your lips.
So that your trust may be in the LORD, I teach you today, even you.
Proverbs 22:17–19

Since Day 1 of this devotional, we've approached the Book of Proverbs one bite at a time, attempting to soak in and apply this vast collection of wisdom piece by piece. And while I assumed at the start that this content would be challenging, I was blissfully ignorant of the struggle that awaited me. What I didn't realize was how tempting (and discouraging) it would be for the achiever in me to assume the role of jury and judge by critically assigning myself a grade for each proverb that we've covered, either pass or fail. Truth be told, along the way, I've felt like I've been doing more *failing* than *becoming*.

Thankfully, however, passages like our key verse for today snap me out of performance mode and realign my heart back to the intended spirit of this important book.

With his hand on our shoulder, we hear the gentle words of our good teacher once again (allow me to paraphrase), "My child, pay attention to what I'm saying. Align your thoughts to these truths. Etch them on your heart (for strength and guidance), and speak them from your lips (to strengthen and guide others). They are for your good."

> For I'm releasing these words to you this day, yes, even to you, so that your living hope will be found in God alone, for he is the only one who is always true. (Proverbs 22:19 TPT)

Tucked away in these verses is the why of all the proverbs: to deepen our trust and point us to more of Jesus, the only One who is always true. The Book of Proverbs wasn't meant to be a merciless beating stick, pointing and poking at our every shortcoming. Instead, it was written *for* us — to remind us of our desperate need of Jesus.

When we're looking for wisdom and don't know what to do — when we're consumed with self and exhausted from living life on our own — when we blow our top and spew all over our loved ones — when we're caught in the middle of a nasty circle of gossip — when our emotions bark orders and attempt to hold us hostage — when we feel alone and in need of a friend — when we feel ourselves bucking against authority — when we're tempted to nag and complain to our husband — when we're overwhelmed and exhausted by the task of training our children — when our skin sags and our waist bulges more than it used to — when pressures rise because the bank account is low — when we lack for nothing materially but still feel unsatisfied — when we're consumed with others' opinions and can't say no — when we feel like we are what we do and nothing more ...

For all these situations and so many more, the Book of Proverbs reminds us that above all else, we need the living, breathing, saving presence of Jesus at work in everything we do.

Like the rest of the Bible, the Book of Proverbs isn't a book to be mastered. Instead, it's an endless source of wisdom to glean from for the rest of our days.

My prayer is that through these pages, the Lord has drawn you in, whet your appetite, and placed in you an insatiable desire for His Word that can't be quenched. And as you turn the page today, I hope you feel encouraged and inspired to return to Proverbs again for the start of something new.

GRAB YOUR FORK

In three words, describe your journey through the Book of Proverbs over these last 30 days.

Of the six topics we touched on (wisdom, pride, words, emotions, relationships, identity), which was most challenging for you?

As you think back through the last 30 days, how has the Book of Proverbs strengthened your faith and pointed you to more of Jesus?

PRAYER

Father, thank You for entrusting to us wisdom from the Book of Proverbs. We confess to You we have so much to learn, and we need You. We can't walk the way of wisdom without You. Please continue to grow in us a desire for more of You. Draw us back to these proverbs, we pray, and through them, deepen our trust. Don't let us miss out on becoming more like You!

HUNGRY FOR MORE?

For me, following Jesus looks like walking with Him to the next right thing. So, as we close out this devotional together, what is that next right thing for you?

For some, your next right thing is to place your trust in Jesus. If somewhere along the way you realized that although you believe in Jesus, you've never actually placed your trust in Him, don't wait another day. Pray this prayer with me.

Jesus, thank You for the endless ways Your love has pursued me. Today I choose to place my faith and hope in You alone. Teach me daily how to depend on and rest in You. You can have all of me, Jesus. I trust in You.

If you prayed that prayer for the first time, tell a trusted friend, and let them celebrate with and encourage you. If you don't have anyone to tell, I'll celebrate with you! You can email me anytime at carriedrogers@gmail.com.

For others, consider the following challenge as your possible next right thing.

Proverbs Challenge

PART 1: READ ONE CHAPTER OF PROVERBS A DAY.

In this devotional, we barely scratched the surface of this profound and practical book, so the first challenge is simple: Read the entire book for yourself.

There are 31 chapters in the Book of Proverbs — one for each day of the month. Whether you decide to start in the middle of the month or want to wait until the first, commit to reading one chapter per day for the next 31 days.

PART 2: DIG INTO ONE PROVERB (ONE VERSE) EACH DAY USING THE SOAP STUDY METHOD.

I think it's safe to say that most believing women don't know how to study the Bible on their own. We depend on our preachers and teachers to do the heavy lifting for us. We need a devotional or Bible study book to guide us into Truth. While these tools are instrumental in our growing faith, they cannot and will not ever replace the importance of going to the Good Book for ourselves.

So just as we've done in this devotional, I want to encourage you to chew on these proverbs one bite at a time for yourselves. As you read through each chapter, pick one proverb a day to dig into using the SOAP study method.

In the pages that follow, I will explain the SOAP method, give you an example of how to SOAP, and provide pages for you to practice for yourself.

You, my friend, can do this. The best way to learn something new is to practice, so pick up your fork and dig in! Jesus will be with you every step of the way. Look to Him, lean on Him, and let Him keep transforming you from the inside out, one baby step at a time, as you walk out this lifelong journey of becoming.

WEEK SIX: *Recap and Reflection*

DAY 26

A woman who invests in her inward beauty far surpasses the one who puts her faith in her fading outward beauty.

DAY 27

Money cannot satisfy and will not last forever, so trust in the Lord, not in your finances.

DAY 28

We can't simultaneously fear God and live to please people.

DAY 29

We are called to commit our work to the Lord, relinquishing the reins of control and working in service to Him.

DAY 30

The Book of Proverbs was written to grow our faith and point us to more dependence on Jesus.

What did you learn about God this week?

How does this truth point you to Jesus?

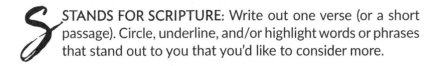

The SOAP Bible Study Method

The S.O.A.P. Method is a simple approach to meditating on one verse of Scripture at a time. I love it because although loose in structure, it provides enough framework to dig as deep as we desire. Here's how it works:

S STANDS FOR SCRIPTURE: Write out one verse (or a short passage). Circle, underline, and/or highlight words or phrases that stand out to you that you'd like to consider more.

O STANDS FOR OBSERVATION: Now it's time to pay attention to what the author is saying in the text. What do you see in this verse? What is the context in which the verse was written? Who was the original audience? What's the overall intended message of the verse? This is also a good time to look up the verse in multiple translations and define any key words. You may also want to practice rewriting the verse in your own words. (Biblegateway.com is a great resource for flipping through different translations of the Bible. Biblehub.com is a great resource for word studies and commentaries.)

A STANDS FOR APPLICATION: Now you are ready to apply the text. How can you apply these truths to your life? How can you put the Word into action today? How does this verse impact your thoughts, words, attitude, and actions? I usually ask myself questions to help apply what I'm reading.

 STANDS FOR PRAYER: Last, turn your application into prayer. Talk to the Lord about the truths you've learned.

S O A P
BIBLE STUDY METHOD
Proverbs 1 (sample)

S For the _waywardness_ of the simple will kill them, and the _complacency_ of fools will destroy them; but _whoever listens to me_ will live in safety and be at ease, without fear of harm. (Proverbs 1:32–33)

O Key words:

waywardness – turning away from the Lord

Complacency – ease, self-satisfaction

Whoever – open invitation to all

Listens to me – listening implies obedience, all who obey

Like an idiot you've turned away from me and chosen destruction instead. Your self-satisfied smugness will kill you. But the one who always listens to me will live undisturbed in a heavenly peace. Free from fear, confident and courageous, you will rest unafraid and sheltered from the storms of life. (TPT)

When we turn away from the Lord, choosing our own way instead of obedience to Him, we are choosing the way of destruction, and ultimately death. But when we obey the Lord and place our lives in His capable hands, we can rest confident and secure.

A In what areas of your life are you turning away from the Lord or choosing to go your own way? Wake up! Living your own way only leads to destruction. How can you practice a continual turning to the Lord throughout the day? Practice this! Don't get comfortable (and complacent) in your day-to-day. Lean in — listen and obey — and He will keep you at peace, confident and secure.

P Father God, remind me throughout the day to continually turn my heart toward You. Wake me up to the areas of my life where I've fallen asleep or become complacent. I want to live my life in humble obedience to You.

S O A P
BIBLE STUDY METHOD

SCRIPTURE

OBSERVATION

APPLICATION

PRAYER

SOAP

BIBLE STUDY METHOD

SCRIPTURE

OBSERVATION

APPLICATION

PRAYER

S O A P

BIBLE STUDY METHOD

SCRIPTURE

OBSERVATION

APPLICATION

PRAYER

S O A P
BIBLE STUDY METHOD

SCRIPTURE

OBSERVATION

APPLICATION

PRAYER

S O A P
BIBLE STUDY METHOD

SCRIPTURE

OBSERVATION

APPLICATION

PRAYER

S O A P
BIBLE STUDY METHOD

SCRIPTURE

OBSERVATION

APPLICATION

PRAYER

S O A P
BIBLE STUDY METHOD

SCRIPTURE

OBSERVATION

APPLICATION

PRAYER

SOAP
BIBLE STUDY METHOD

SCRIPTURE

OBSERVATION

APPLICATION

PRAYER

S O A P
BIBLE STUDY METHOD

SCRIPTURE

OBSERVATION

APPLICATION

PRAYER

S O A P
BIBLE STUDY METHOD

SCRIPTURE

OBSERVATION

APPLICATION

PRAYER

S O A P
BIBLE STUDY METHOD

SCRIPTURE

OBSERVATION

APPLICATION

PRAYER

S O A P
BIBLE STUDY METHOD

SCRIPTURE

OBSERVATION

APPLICATION

PRAYER

S O A P
BIBLE STUDY METHOD

SCRIPTURE

OBSERVATION

APPLICATION

PRAYER

S O A P
BIBLE STUDY METHOD

SCRIPTURE

OBSERVATION

APPLICATION

PRAYER

S O A P
BIBLE STUDY METHOD

SCRIPTURE

OBSERVATION

APPLICATION

PRAYER

S O A P
BIBLE STUDY METHOD

SCRIPTURE

OBSERVATION

APPLICATION

PRAYER

S O A P
BIBLE STUDY METHOD

SCRIPTURE

OBSERVATION

APPLICATION

PRAYER

S O A P
BIBLE STUDY METHOD

SCRIPTURE

OBSERVATION

APPLICATION

PRAYER

SOAP

BIBLE STUDY METHOD

SCRIPTURE

OBSERVATION

APPLICATION

PRAYER

S O A P
BIBLE STUDY METHOD

SCRIPTURE

OBSERVATION

APPLICATION

PRAYER

S O A P
BIBLE STUDY METHOD

SCRIPTURE

OBSERVATION

APPLICATION

PRAYER

SOAP
BIBLE STUDY METHOD

SCRIPTURE

OBSERVATION

APPLICATION

PRAYER

S O A P
BIBLE STUDY METHOD

SCRIPTURE

OBSERVATION

APPLICATION

PRAYER

S O A P
BIBLE STUDY METHOD

SCRIPTURE

OBSERVATION

APPLICATION

PRAYER

S O A P
BIBLE STUDY METHOD

SCRIPTURE

OBSERVATION

APPLICATION

PRAYER

SOAP
BIBLE STUDY METHOD

SCRIPTURE

OBSERVATION

APPLICATION

PRAYER

S O A P

BIBLE STUDY METHOD

SCRIPTURE

OBSERVATION

APPLICATION

PRAYER

S O A P
BIBLE STUDY METHOD

SCRIPTURE

OBSERVATION

APPLICATION

PRAYER

S O A P

BIBLE STUDY METHOD

SCRIPTURE

OBSERVATION

APPLICATION

PRAYER

S O A P
BIBLE STUDY METHOD

SCRIPTURE

OBSERVATION

APPLICATION

PRAYER

S O A P
BIBLE STUDY METHOD

SCRIPTURE

OBSERVATION

APPLICATION

PRAYER

OTHER BOOKS BY THE AUTHOR

HE IS ...: KNOWING GOD BY NAME
{10-week Bible study}

In the Bible, God reveals Himself through His many names — names that reveal more clearly who He is and how He works in our lives. To know God's names is to know God. In *He Is ...: Knowing God by Name*, author Carrie Rogers invites you to look deeply into the character of God as she introduces 11 of His names. This 10-week study offers you an intimate approach to knowing God by name. In the process, you will be wooed and wowed by the stunning power, perfection, and presence found in each of His names.

THE WARDROBE OF CHRIST: PUTTING ON THE CHARACTER OF JESUS
{6-week Bible study}

Are you walking around each day spiritually naked, unprepared to face the challenges and temptations of the day? Have you given much thought to what is hanging in your spiritual closet? Just as you get dressed each day physically, you are also called to clothe yourself spiritually. In *The Wardrobe of Christ: Putting On the Character of Jesus*, author Carrie Rogers provides an in-depth look at what it means to clothe yourself with Jesus. By examining each virtue listed in Colossians 3:12–14, you will discover that in Christ, you can put on compassion, kindness, humility, gentleness, patience, forgiveness, and love.

A MEANINGFUL CHRISTMAS: A 24-DAY DEVOTIONAL FOR WOMEN

Amid the hustle and bustle of the holiday season, *A Meaningful Christmas* provides a simple approach for women to focus on the true meaning of Christmas. My prayer is that this little book will be a breath of fresh air in your chaotic day and a time to focus your heart and mind on Jesus — our Savior, Messiah, and King.

SEEDS: SCRIPTURE PRAYERS FOR YOUR FAMILY

Welcome to *Seeds*, a little book of Scripture prayers for you and your family. The prayers written in this book are broken into three categories: prayers for your man, prayers for your littles, and prayers for you. It's my prayer that these words become a starting place of prayer for you on behalf of the ones you hold most dear.

www.CarriedAwayMinistries.com

Made in the USA
Coppell, TX
13 February 2023

12717449R00096